THIRTY YEARS WITH AN IDEA

Marietta Johnson

MARIETTA JOHNSON

Thirty Years
with an Idea

Published for the Organic School
Fairhope, Alabama
by
THE UNIVERSITY OF ALABAMA PRESS
University, Alabama

To the individuals, parents, teachers, businessmen,
and organizations that, over the years, have sustained
the Marietta Johnson School of Organic Education.

CONTENTS

PREFACE

The publication of *Thirty Years with an Idea* by Marietta Johnson is a tribute to the importance of an idea about education. The school which she started 67 years ago continues, today, to keep her thinking alive and its campus active as it has through two world wars and an economic depression.

This book is a reflection of the mind of one woman and those countless lives in which she aroused a curiosity about the world.

What began as an educational experiment based on common sense about the nature of the growing child has endured to prove its validity as an approach to education. It is supported by later physiological and psychological discoveries concerning human growth and development.

Marietta Johnson finished writing *Thirty Years with an Idea* shortly before her death in 1938. Today the "new" trend in educational thinking makes the publication of Mrs. Johnson's book even more appropriate. Educators are rediscovering and expressing much of the same philosophy upon which she founded her school more than two generations ago.

BOARD OF DIRECTORS
MARIETTA JOHNSON
SCHOOL OF ORGANIC EDUCATION
FAIRHOPE, ALABAMA

FOREWORD

The idea herein described is a very important one that has had a long hard road, and is yet not firmly established in schools. It is a simple fact of life, proved over and over again, and accepted in theory, so it would seem unnecessary to bring out a book about it in 1974. But, in reality, this idea is needed now even more than it was needed in 1907, for problems increase with population. That the natural laws of human growth must be understood, respected, and used, if the child is to become a well-developed, well-rounded individual sounds easy to understand. Why is it difficult? It is just as easy and difficult as it is for us to obey natural laws about our other limited resources. Man has a way of feeling superior to natural laws, and the educator belongs to man's world. With the very best intentions, he has felt it more important to hold the child to external standards than to inner ones. And it is much easier to mold the child after his own pattern than to help him grow from within.

Marietta Johnson tells here how difficult it was for her to accept even thinking about it, for it would mean she would have to change, and she liked the system she was working under. She enjoyed getting children to work harder and harder to meet the standards, praising and rejoicing with them when they succeeded. But, after reading Nathan Oppenheim's THE DEVELOPMENT OF THE CHILD, she reluctantly agreed that change she must. The scientists had discovered that the child was not a 'little adult', but a growing organism that went through stages that should be recognized by educators. For example, they reported that the nervous system grows slowly—so slowly, in fact, that in the first eight years of life any activity requiring fine adjustments of eye and hand muscles could cause undue strain and nervous exhaustion, hindering growth.

This book tells what else she learned and what she did about it. She didn't start a do-as-you-please school, nor did she give up acquiring knowledge and skills. She had doubts and kept asking herself questions. Shall we ever be able to identify education as growth? Shall we ever recognize health of body, wholesome activity, and sincerity and joy of spirit as education? Then, she dedicated herself to the task of answering those questions with a rousing affirmative.

In 1921 I found my way to The Organic School. I was astonished by the freedom and the openness: children from kindergarten through high school learning because they wanted to, without marks, tests, or prizes; work for work's sake being basic; creativity central to the curriculum instead of peripheral. I entered into teaching there with zest, delighted that I had to join all the creative work going on, on the principle that one couldn't teach any process without having had first-hand experience. I stayed five years and, like many others, acquired the inspiration and confidence I needed for carrying on the ideas in subsequent teaching.

It is impossible for me to assess the influence of this school, and Marietta Johnson herself would be the first to refuse any attempt to measure. We, who learned with her the poem LET ME LOSE COUNT by Laura Spencer Porter, know how strongly she felt on that matter. "All I want" she would say, "is that you put first things first, that you see to it your own growth is wholesome; then you can be honest in working for wholesome growth in children."

In the early years she felt very much alone. Then, simultaneously, in widespread areas in the United States and Europe, schools like hers began to spring up, manned by people reacting to the scientists' findings, the education-is-growth idea. Since she traveled widely in order to get financial support for the school, she sought out these people and was tremendously encouraged. She reveled in the growth of the progressive movement and the effort of schools in general to put more wholesome conditions for growth into their programs—The Gary Plan, The Winnetka Plan, The Dalton Plan, and the work of experimental schools of the universities.

Today the Open Classrooms are out on the growing edge. Their brochures show that they are taking natural laws seriously: "The child learns best when given freedom to explore the world around him with a minimum of direction." "The teacher's function is not to present answers, or questions, but instead to provide opportunities within which he will generate his own questions, and from which he will derive his own answers." "He has a right to elect what he will do and what he shall be; he has the obligation to preserve similar rights for others." This describes what Marietta Johnson was driving at—the privilege to BE.

There has been appreciable growth in this kind of educational nourishment, but in terms of need it is nowhere near enough. Thousands of children are still being denied their natural birthright. Since children represent our most valuable resource for the future, it is time for an all-out approach to this massive problem. The more books like this being published, the better.

KENNETT SQUARE, PA.   GRACE ROTZEL
MARCH, 1974

MEMOIR
MARIETTA JOHNSON AND THE
SCHOOL OF ORGANIC EDUCATION

She was a woman holding a lamp for the feet of children. Thus I introduce to you Marietta Pierce Johnson, founder of the School of Organic Education in Fairhope, Alabama. In the field of education, she was a pioneer, a visionary, and a demonstration center for the belief that "education is identical with growth." She called her school "Organic" because it was designed to meet the needs of the growing organism. She felt that no requirements should be made for entrance into any school; not "What do you know?" but "What do you need?" should be the question, and the school should be able to supply that need.

Marietta Louise Pierce was born in St. Paul, Minnesota in 1864, daughter of Clarence and Rhoda Morton Pierce, who had moved west from New York State. She was graduated from the State Normal School in St. Cloud, Minnesota, in 1885, and taught in the St. Paul Teachers' Training School and other State Teachers' Colleges in Minnesota. In 1897 she married John Franklin Johnson of St. Paul. They had two sons, Clifford and Franklin, and lived on a small ranch. They decided to move south, as the cold winters were affecting Mrs. Johnson's health, and wrote to a friend in Fairhope, Alabama to look around and buy a pecan grove for them. The friend wrote back, "Come down and buy it yourself."

So in 1907 they came to Fairhope, in Baldwin County, and now Alabama can proudly claim this remarkable woman for its very own. For here she lived the rest of her life; here she founded her School of Organic Education; from here she traveled all over America and Europe presenting her progressive and revolutionary educational doctrines.

Photographs of Marietta Johnson reveal her as a quietly beautiful woman, with softly waved hair, fine penetrating eyes. There is serenity and competence in her face, and her brown eyes seem to shine with warmth and humor. She was also a woman dedicated to an ideal—a better way of education for children—and she pursued this ideal with strength and conviction all her life. It gave her an added beauty.

Marietta Johnson tells the story of her "conversion" to what was to become her life work in the following words: "I was teaching in a normal school in the Middle West," she begins. "I was young and full of enthusiasm for my profession, sure that the hope of democracy lay in universal education, and that I was helping to build a better world. I wanted to give the children as much as they could possibly do, and I was working out new ways of teaching whereby they could get through four First Readers in three months." She shook her head with a shamefaced smile. "It was a fine example of the factory system at its worst," she confessed. "Of course, I didn't know any better then, but just the same, it makes me feel like a criminal every time I think of it now. Then one day my superintendent handed me a thick red book, and said: "Unless education shifts its course to conform with these discoveries, it cannot expect to hold the attention of the best of you young teachers." I was startled, and appalled, but I took the book home and read it. It was Nathaniel Oppenheim's *Development of the Child* and it changed my entire scheme of thinking and teaching.

"I discovered that I had been forcing children 'way beyond their powers, that I had practically been maiming their minds and emotions, and that the entire system under which I taught went

directly contrary to the natural needs of the child. I determined to
do no more teaching until I knew more about children, and for
several years I worked and studied, trying to find out what
children needed, and what sort of environment would make for
their finest growth." It was when she had studied "Education and
the Larger Life" by Charles Manford Henderson that she felt she
had something practical upon which to start, and with her own
small boys she began to experiment. They were too young for
schooling, but not for education.

She had the opportunity to put her theories into further
practice when the Johnsons came to live in the Single Tax Colony
at Fairhope, Alabama. Here in this small community of culti-
vated, thinking people, believers in the Henry George theory that
all men are equally entitled to the use of the earth, Marietta
Johnson found herself in an atmosphere congenial and receptive
to her unusual abilities. In the summer of 1907, Mr. and Mrs.
H. S. Comings asked her to open a free school for young
children, offering to provide $25 a month for expenses. She
happily accepted, rented a small cottage for $15 a month, and had
$10 left for her salary and supplies for her six pupils.

Such was the modest beginning of an educational experiment
which eventually attracted the interest of many educators here
and abroad. Classes were added from year to year until a
complete system of primary, grammar, and secondary schooling
was developed, a two-year training course for teachers, and a
six-weeks course for parents of students.

The young students in the Organic School had no desks or
books, they were given no marks, report cards, or examinations.
They were grouped according to age, the work being adapted to
the stage of development of the group, and individual attention
given when necessary. Classes were often held out of doors, and a
sandstone gully near the school was a fine place for arithmetic
lessons—the red clay walls made an excellent blackboard, and a
stick or a stone a good pencil.

Her students learned, for she taught them well. Graduates of
the Organic School had two years of Latin and French; four years
of science, which included biology, botany, physics, and chemistry; four years of history; two years of arts and crafts and

woodworking; a thorough knowledge of outdoor nature, of folk singing and dancing. Above all, she taught them poise, courtesy, and manners, and a remarkable lack of self-consciousness.

John Dewey of Columbia University was invited to come to Fairhope and investigate the school. In his book, "Schools of Tomorrow," he devoted an entire chapter to the Marietta Johnson school. His favorable report was of inestimable value, not only in establishing it in the minds of educators and others, but also in serving as a great help in securing funds. For much of Marietta Johnson's time and energy was spent in raising money for the school. "I've been a beggar all these years," she said, and she so impressed Joseph Fels, the naphtha soap millionaire, that he early gave $11,000 to her school!

It had been said that the Organic School was better known in Europe than in the United States, and better known in other states than in Alabama. Marietta Johnson was invited to lecture at the New Educational Fellowship World Conference at Heidelberg, Germany, in 1925; at Locarno, Switzerland, in 1927; at Dublin, Ireland, in 1933. She was a speaker at the International Girl Scout Conference in Cambridge, England, in 1922, and at the Chicago World's Fair in 1933. She was one of the founders of the Progressive Education Association at Washington, D.C. in 1920, and frequently contributed to its publication, "Progressive Education." Her own book, "Youth in a World of Men," (published by The John Day Co. in 1929) was widely read by educators.

The years of the 1920's reached and maintained a high plateau in Marietta Johnson's national and international recognition. Her ideal of giving each child an opportunity to develop his highest capacity without suffering the devastating pressure of competition began to take hold in other schools: at Caldwell, New Jersey; Port Washington, Long Island; Menlo Park, California; and Pawling, New York.

Perhaps the best known school to follow her principles of teaching was the Edgewood School at Greenwich, Connecticut. The events which led to her association with this school make an amusing story. Mrs. Johnson was traveling by train to a speaking engagement, when she discovered she had rushed off without any money, except for a check. She was talking with the conductor about her dilemma, when a man seated near, overhearing the conversation, introduced himself and offered advice. The man was W. J. Hoggson, of Greenwich, a school trustee very much interested in educational matters.

Mr. Hoggson proved to be a good friend and an influential one. He invited her to speak at his home, and here she met Mrs. Charles D. Lanier, daughter-in-law of the poet, Sidney Lanier, who had just started what she called "The Little School in the Woods" on the Lanier estate nearby. The enthusiasm of Mrs. Lanier and other prominent people in Greenwich resulted in what became the famous Edgewood School. Mrs. Johnson's association with this school continued for 13 years. Many teachers who achieved prominence along progressive education lines received their early training at Edgewood.

The years passed rapidly, for she was forever busy. There were years of incredible hardships, and not without personal tragedy. Her small son, Franklin, was accidentally killed, and in 1919 her husband died. Mr. Johnson's help, encouragement, and assistance with the school had been her mainstay, but this courageous woman still carried on. For thirty-two years she served her school, her children, without pay, except for a simple living in the school home. She contributed unselfishly of her own income, and gave the school all money raised on her lecture tours. Most of all, she gave of herself, and the wholehearted response of her students she considered to be her measure of success, her reward. Her good friend, Mrs. Comings, said of her: "Mrs. Johnson was an inspired speaker and teacher with older people, but with the children she was simply marvelous. They gave her eager and rapt attention, and I have never known her to ask anything of a pupil that she did not get immediate response."

Marietta Johnson died on December 23, 1938. A month earlier, the Alumni Association of the School of Organic Education gave a dinner honoring her at the Colonial Inn, in Fairhope. She was unable to attend, for her overworked heart was giving out. Words of love and appreciation were heaped upon her; tributes and testimonials from those prominent in civic, educational, and professional fields were read; letters and telegrams from near and far poured out a flood of admiration and respect.

From the many tributes, which were preserved in a scrapbook by her friends and presented to Marietta Johnson before her death, we do well to remember this: "We in Alabama are proud of the fact that Mrs. Johnson's life and work have been spent in our state environs; that Mrs. Johnson has found right here in Alabama fertile ground in which to plant the seed of her knowledge and inspiration, so that, under her guidance a newer, more natural, and more perfect standard of education has grown and flourished. In any given century, God gives to this earth only a few of His chosen leaders. We are fortunate that he has placed, in the person of Marietta Johnson, such a one in our midst. We do ourselves honor by honoring her."

FAIRHOPE, ALABAMA   GEORGE ALLEN BROWN

Mr. Brown's Memoir *is published with permission of the Alabama Historical Association, at whose eighteenth annual meeting the memoir was read.*

THIRTY YEARS WITH AN IDEA

First School Building

1 HOW IT BEGAN

I had been a teacher for years. I think I had always been a teacher in my heart. At about ten years of age I began dreaming of the time when I should be a teacher, announcing on all possible occasions, "I am going to be a teacher when I grow up."

I had taught all grades in the elementary school and also had had experience in high school teaching. But most of all I enjoyed my work as a "training teacher" in the city training school and State Teachers College. Their duty was to assign work to the "teachers in training," observe and criticize, sometimes giving special instruction in "methods," as "critic teachers." They had charge of as many as twenty young students, all getting experience as student teachers.

I was always enthusiastic. It was a great joy to me when six-year-old children in the first grade could read through four first readers in three months!! This resulted from a special method of grading the difficulties, teaching phonics, etc. Of course, it was high pressure, but they could do it! The student teachers were thrilled with these results and no doubt went out into teaching positions determined to reach these standards. The parents were pleased. I was a success! And we all truly believed that the children loved to do it, and that it was good for them!

Many, many times since then I have known parents and teachers to defend unwise demands made of children with the claim that the children "love it." Children often "love" to do very unwholesome things! A group of twelve-year-olds became interested in dramatics, and one little girl, a leader, and more talented than the rest, was quite inclined to overdo—working for long periods (and losing sleep)—when she should have been playing, thinking, planning, and composing. It became necessary to divert her attention, to draw her into play and crafts, and help her to forget her literary aspirations. One of the most important duties of the adult is to protect the child from his own ignorance, caprice, or lack of control. This is a part of providing the right conditions for growth. Some of the so-called progressive schools are so devoted to the idea of children leading that they often allow quite unsuitable activities.

At that time, the method employed received favorable attention. In fact, I enjoyed some little distinction, and was interviewed by book agents requesting commendation of their texts. The children were enthusiastic and were stimulated to greater efforts. The greater the effort, the more I rejoiced and praised the children! "Johnnie is learning to read very rapidly," reported a fond mother. "I can't keep him away from his books!" "That's splendid," replied the teacher. If the teacher had been wise she would have advised the mother to provide all sorts of creative material and to encourage the child to use them—drawing him away from books—explaining to the mother the danger of specialized activity for young children. Overspecialization tends to arrest development even in adults, says a child specialist, and adds, "All specialization may be overspecialization for the child."

Occasionally a child might become nearsighted, or be taken out of school because of nervousness. This, of course, was a grief to me, because my personal relation to children was always one of informal good-fellowship. I loved children—or thought I did—and wished them to be well and happy, but it never occurred to me that the work of the school was really unwise. I should have resented the idea that we were pushing the children. Parents and teachers do not realize that allowing children to engage in activities belonging to a later stage *is* pushing them! Parents often allow their children to "speak pieces," play instruments, and participate at evening functions with adults. If, as sometimes happened, a child was too ill or undeveloped to do all the work required in a certain grade, we were too loyal to the system to allow him to 'pass'. The other children in the group would have resented allowing children to continue who had not "done the work!"

The Curriculum was sacred! To be an honest teacher meant to insist upon every child meeting the requirements or being considered a failure! No favoritism was ever allowed.

To fail, of course, meant to remain in the lower class while one's classmates were promoted. It never occured to us to question the requirements, or to entertain the idea for a moment that we had failed!! I had not heard then of the injurious effects of self-depreciation—of the sinking of spirit which children might suffer—nor the danger of developing the inferiority complex.

It still amazes me to see quite able—at least, very successful—teachers, keeping "honor" rolls, giving awards for scholarship, attendance, etc., even when quite conscious of the fundamental evils of such a system! Self-consciousness is acknowledged to be a great barrier to the growth of power! Since *human power* is the great objective of all study and instruction, why should we tolerate a system of grading and rewards that develops and emphasizes self-consciousness—definitely undermining human power!

I loved children. I have since learned, however, that true love of children is measured by one's ability to meet their need even to the point of self-effacement. Many adults show their affection for children by playing with them, fondling them, and drawing them out in conversation, etc. Few are able to enjoy children at a distance! Children were never afraid of me. They approached me freely and I am sure were perfectly confident of my good will. Many people argue that the method or aim of the school is not as important as the personality of the teacher. I insist that the finest personality may ignorantly—though lovingly—do the wrong thing! While happiness is fundamental, still children may be happy doing quite undesirable things, and teachers of strong personalities and great enthusiasm may do the greatest harm. Froebel says that "ambitious parents and high-pressure teachers continue to destroy the power they are set to conserve." A little boy, very conscious of his high scholastic standing, was unable to associate with other children happily. He was critical and demanding, self-conscious and egotistical—and the other children withdrew from him. When he complained that the children would not play with him, the teacher asked, "What is the matter with you? Are you too bossy? Perhaps, if you did not read so much and paid more attention to the other children, you might learn how to play with them."

A little girl ready for eighth grade was put in her age group and gradually developed a simpler, more direct attitude—to the joy of her parents and the delight of her teachers. At first she was inclined to be unhappy and felt superior to the children of her age—but presently in the atmosphere of freedom she became acquainted with the other children and took keen delight in playing in an unsophisticated, child-like way. "Virtue itself turn vice, being misapplied." Sometimes we find what is often called a poor teacher, but I am comforted with the thought that if the teacher does not teach much, at least no harm is being done and life does something for the children. If we could only cultivate the seeing eye we should be amazed at the development taking place even where there is little or no instruction.

I enjoyed a measure of success and used to pity those who had never taught school. It was the most thrilling work I could imagine. It still is the most thrilling work in the world. It is true that many teachers do not find it thrilling, but this is when the work is mechanicalized by external standards. The inner standard preserves the creative character of all teaching! To watch the unfolding organism—to recognize growing intelligence—to witness the joy and eagerness of children employed in wholesome activity—to observe them at play and in self-prompted occupation—to observe the growth and skill and see the satisfaction in the faces of the children—is one of the greatest privileges of the adult. The external standard robs the child of spontaneity and robs the teacher of the most precious experience that can come to her—the creative element in teaching! A little boy coming from a conventional school carried books to and from school, to "keep track" of the work lest he fall behind his grade in the home school. The mother constantly compared his work with what he would have done had he remained at home, and urged him to work hard to "keep up!" That was a real tragedy to the child. He never felt free to play heartily with the children—in fact, he was being robbed of childhood.

During my work as a critic, my superintendent thrust a book into my hand one day, saying: "Unless education takes this direction, there is no incentive for a young man to enter the profession." This was a great shock to me. I felt there was every incentive for everybody to enter the profession. I was mystified to think that education must change its *direction.* I had never objected to the system. I had always followed it with enthusiasm and felt that more knowledge and greater consecration was all that could be desired. I used to attend educational conventions and summer schools to improve my method, and studied constantly to improve my scholarship. I have listened to learned professors exhort young teachers to study to know more, to take courses and degrees, to get credentials—and I felt that the ability to use the latest method was the only sign of progress in the profession. To my mind, the child was being educated if he was acquiring knowledge and skill and learning to behave well—and the teacher an educator if he had the ability to impart knowledge, to direct and control, and to insist upon "attainment and achievement." Strange that many of us are still measuring education in these terms!! Shall we ever be able to identify education as growth? Shall we ever recognize health of body, wholesome mental activity and sincerity and joy of spirit as education? Think of the army of teachers attending summer schools, studying for a higher degree, better salaries. Of course, they should study and have better salaries, but the joy of knowing—the thrill of intellectual stimulation—becoming better human beings—is the real reward.

One prominent leader used to point his finger at the group of teachers and shriek: "Can you *think* through the subject?" Of course, no one could think through the subject, but these leaders insisted that a good teacher must know "subject matter from A to Z." Very little was said in those days about the *needs of childhood!* "The person who knows his way through the woods is better able to pilot others through them," explained one learned gentleman. His only idea of education seemed to be that of piloting children through the various subjects listed in the curriculum. We often hear complaints about the lack of personality in teachers. May this not be due to the external demands they have to meet and must still meet, and also to the external demands they are forced to put upon their pupils? "Subject matter" is still considered the most important thing in education. Occasionally, we do hear some fond parent say, "I do not care so much what my child *learns,* but I want him to know how to live with others, to develop initiative, and lose his hesitancy and self-consciousness." And yet, these very parents often insist upon strong intellectual stimulation indicated by advanced work in science or mathematics.

Of course, in a general way, we were taught as student teachers that children should not be afraid, that they should be happy, but *learn* they must, and we believed that a teacher's success was measured by the academic progress of the pupils. We still hear of pupils failing or being conditioned in subjects, but how often do we hear of pupils being retained because of undeveloped social or moral qualities? When children became indifferent or resisted instruction, we sometimes changed the method, but usually blamed the children! The course of study must be administered, the standard must be reached, the only problem was: "How can it be done most easily?" In many modern schools, one finds new methods, new devices, but the persistence of the old standard. The attainment and achievement tests; the scoring of the work by the children themselves—all of this tends to develop self-consciousness. Some of the most distressing cases of self-consciousness are sometimes found in the "progressive" schools where children are delegated to "show the visitor" the work and make explanations. The point of view of following a course of study seemed perfectly right to me and I was surprised at the idea that education could or should change its direction. I went home and read the book given to me by my superintendent. It was Nathan Oppenheim's *Development of the Child.* This book has been my inspiration ever since. It was also my despair, because it made me feel that I was a child destroyer, whereas I had rejoiced in the thought that my work was good for children and acceptable to society. I discovered that nearly everything I had been doing with such pride and success in the primary department was a violation of the order of the development of the nervous system. I realized that my enthusiasm was destructive, and the more efficient I was, the more I injured the pupils!

I learned that we were teaching altogether too much and that most of it was quite unnecessary and unsuited to the child, if not positively harmful to him. I learned that children should not be put at books until at least ten years of age, and that most of the work of the primary school should be postponed until a later time. Most people are shocked at postponing formal work and ask, "What will you have them do? Don't you want them to *learn* anything?" One of the greatest authorities in child study points out that much of the work in the primary school is too severe a form of specialized activity to be wholesome for young children.

The Development of the Child became my educational Bible, and its frequent perusal has been a marvelous stimulation and support through many years of experimental work.

I began to see the child in an entirely different light —began to realize that he is unformed, unripe, imma- ture—that he is in no condition even to be trained. "Train- ing" and "growing" are quite different. In training, we often dominate or force in order to accomplish certain definite external results. In growing, we provide the right conditions and the end is human and immediate—included in the process—and the moving power is within! If the child is wholesomely, happily, intelligently employed, he *is* being educated!

The tremendous increase in weight in the first fifteen years of life means that changes are taking place so rapidly that great care must be used to avoid arrest of development. Arrest of development is well-nigh universal. Most of us meet social situations in a most immature way. Sometimes I think we have all "grown-up" physically and intellectually, but socially and spiritually, we are still infants.

There are broad avenues of waste in this condition of rapid change and the main business of the adult is the conservation of childhood. There are many efforts being made by philanthropic individuals and groups to help children. If we could establish economic justice and the schools concentrated upon providing the right conditions of growth, all of the charitable efforts would be almost if not quite, unnecessary!

Nathan Oppenheim says:

The child whose sense of right is wrongly or too early taxed, whose power of food assimilation is abused, whose order of mental development is ignored, is suffering from poor nutrition. The child who prematurely participates in experience and ways of living, who is allowed to wander outside of the limits that a conservative idea of growth imposes, who becomes subject to conditions that only the strength of maturity can withstand, is thus subjected to adverse conditions that must surely leave their mark upon his later organic form. (How often parents and teachers are guilty of subjecting the child, in study, work, discipline, and even in play, to such conditions!) Such a child is suffering from a vicious nutrition. The child who assumes responsibilities beyond his years, who undergoes the wear and tear attending the course of a too-rapid development, who lacks the benefits of a wise restraint and discipline, is bound to show the effects in a partial and one-sided development that bars him out from the full beauty of finished maturity. Such a child suffers from the effects of a misdirected and vicious nutrition.

"Nutrition" here covers every item that influences growth and does not refer merely to food.

The main work of the child is to grow. To be able to recognize the signs of growth in children of any age is a great art! One must study the results of the experts—must respect the findings of authorities—and then one must study at first hand the reaction of children. No one need ever hope to know perfectly, the signs of a languishing or flourishing child, but it is the blessed privilege of parents, teachers, and all adults to *try* to *know*. Only by meeting the demands of growth may we hope for normal children and later normal adult life. This is the peculiar responsibility of education. We do not claim to have a new method—nor a system—but merely a different point of view—that of emphasizing the effects on the children of all activities and exercises of the school. We also endeavor to influence the home. Instead of being taught facts, children should be helped to understand their experiences.

The more I studied the book, the more appalled I became at what I had been doing. I went back to my superintendent saying, "The scales are off. If ever I have a child of my own, whose education I can control, he will not be put at books until he is at least ten years of age."

The child does not need reading in his business of growing, and while he may not become nearsighted immediately, such work subjects him to strain which should be avoided. All children naturally *think* through experience —through activity. One of the prevalent fallacies is that children are not "thinking" unless occupied with books. In some cases, the book may *prevent* true thinking. A child who uses symbols too early cannot be as clear a thinker as one whose thought is stimulated by doing. A child who learns to read at an early age often sits in a bad light, in a bad position, being entertained when he should be more actively and socially employed.

Too often people take truth on authority—that is, they accept things because of the word of the book or some authority. If the mind were trained to withhold decision until the truth is ascertained and then take that for authority, we should have a saner world.

Little children are not ready for the analysis of symbols which learning to read entails. It is a great strain on the teacher also to try to teach children symbols when they should be using things. The many methods of teaching reading testify to the difficulty of such work. "I tell you, it is hard work to teach these little children to read," exclaimed a doubting principal. "All the more reason it should be postponed," is the reply. A few years later the art of reading may be learned with much less effort, in much less time, and without danger to the nervous system. "If I could direct the learning process later, I should prefer that children do not learn to read until twelve years of age or even older," exclaimed an educated leader.

A young teacher taught a class of eight-year-old children to read. She offered them work which had been outlined for six-year-olds and found that they were able to do a week's work in one day, and a month's work in a week! They were so eager, her only fear was that they might overdo! It is a great saving of energy nerve tissue and time to allow children a few more years in occupations which really minister to growth. It is a pity to waste time; to waste childhood is tragedy! I am sure that older children and adults would profit intellectually by creative occupation with materials. The school should provide what is called "occupational" or "activity work" for students at every stage—but the elementary school child should have less book work. A child who appeared uninterested in books was not pressed to learn to read and did not really acquire the art until thirteen years of age. At fifteen, as a sopho-more in high school, his teachers testified to his being one of the best readers in the class. As one teacher explained, "He reads with more understanding."

I tried to make some changes in my work immediately, but it was difficult. The system was established, and formal work was expected of the children six and seven years of age.

However, I began agitating and read eagerly everything I could find about the development of the child. This book of Nathan Oppenheim's is on the shelves of every Teachers College of this country. Strange that its findings have not made a greater impression on the primary school process! G. W. T. Patrick, of the University of Iowa, has made a notable contribution to this subject in a monograph entitled *Should Children Read or Write under Ten Years of Age.* Some of the later scientists and students of human development are in hearty accord with Oppenheim's theory. He pointed out the nature and the need of childhood, and while he criticized what the schools were doing, he did not offer a substitute program.

Later, C. Manford Henderson, in his epoch-making book, *Education and the Larger Life,* presented a most constructive criticism of life and education. He not only agreed with Oppenheim as to the nature of the growing child and the insistence that the adult's supreme responsi-bility is to supply the right conditions of growth, but suggested a practical program—life-giving to body, mind, and spirit.

This idea took possession of me and I could not rest until I had started a school. I began experimenting with my own child and other children of the neighborhood, in the country where we were living. My effort was to try to find a way for children to learn as much as *I thought* they should learn without external pressure. I still entertained the attainment-achievement idea!! I did not want my child to grow up ignorant. I wished him to be a credit to the family! It is strange that parents and teachers are still unable to recognize "learning" except in the conscious effort of doing so. Dewey speaks of the "conscious job of learning" as of less importance than we think. And usually "learning" implies the use of books! As a matter of fact, learning is something that happens to one in the course of an experience! We have splendid authority for the idea of *doing* in order to know. Even to this day, many people desire tangible, measurable results!

At first, I accepted the usual standard, struggling to find a better method, but experience persuaded me to discard external standards altogether and work for an inner, human one. The teacher must learn to *detect* when children are wholesomely occupied—that is, doing their best—and should find a way to secure this best. The teacher must know the specific powers of the individual student and provide conditions for the highest use of these powers.

It is not easy for a teacher to judge her work by the spontaneity, interest, and joy of the children, rather than by information and skill. I am sure we may safely seek the "kingdom" that is human fineness and that these other things—that is, knowledge and skill—will be added. In fact, knowledge and skill are inevitable. But we are constantly measuring the child's work by some adult or near-adult standard. The inner standard is one that the school must meet, not one to be imposed on the children. It is that of providing conditions which strengthen and vivify the physical being, enlist the finest use of the mental endowment, and preserve the sincerity and joy of the emotional life.

No doubt, it will still take a long time for the educational system to accept this standard. Much of our most modern work is designed to increase information and skill. I always shiver a little when I see children anxious to show their knowledge and skill to visitors: "I made this myself. I designed it without any help," exclaimed a ten-year-old. And the mother, beaming happily, in a stage whisper says, "how beautifully unself-conscious!"

There are many excellent elementary schools where a real effort is made to meet the needs of childhood, but the standards of entrance into high school and college continue to be the "most disastrous obstacle." Surely the time is not far distant when elementary schools will be able to concentrate unreservedly upon the present needs of the child, the higher institutions devoting themselves to meeting the needs at a later stage.

Wouldn't it be wonderful if high schools and colleges dared to take the children as they *are* and minister unto them? If they dared do this, they would without doubt find a finer human product of the high schools knocking at their doors.

In the summer of 1907, Mr. and Mrs. W. S. Comings, of Fairhope, asked me to come and open a free school, offering to provide twenty-five dollars a month. I had been in Fairhope some years before and was longing to return. There is a saying that any one who visits Fairhope long enough to get Baldwin County sand in his shoes must eventually return. I was fully committed to the idea of starting school and gladly embraced this opportunity. I was so anxious to "try out" the idea that I should have been willing to pay children to come and let me experiment. So, I accepted the twenty-five dollars per month, renting a cottage for fifteen, leaving ten dollars per month for salary and supplies! Six children came the first day. I did not know what to do. There was nothing in my previous experience as a teacher to throw light upon my path. I had always had a course of study to follow and my main problem had been to find the best way to administer the curriculum. I had not been trained to look for results in eagerness of attack, in spontaneous activity, in the growth of initiative—bright eyes, healthy satisfactions. "Subject matter" had always referred to knowledge and skill acquired. Now I had no course of study. I must work from a new point of view. Our school has always been an effort to work with children from the point of view of meeting their needs rather than getting them to meet the demands of any system. Not "what do they know" but "how do they grow" is our slogan. The school must provide conditions under which every child may flourish, none languish. After all, if childhood is the unformed period in the development of the individual, isn't it natural that the educational process should be employed in ministering to that stage?

To be able to recognize the signs of health of body, mind, and spirit is a great accomplishment not easily acquired. From this point of view, the teacher learns the meaning of life as revealed in children's activity. It is the most creative, fascinating, exacting work in which any adult may engage.

I had always judged a school by questioning: What do they know? Have they covered the ground? Are they thorough? What can they do? Are they accurate and skillful, and is their response rapid and sure? How do they behave? Do they mind their own affairs and study as they should? Do they concentrate on the work assigned?

The questions now pressing were: Am I providing suitable work for children of this age? Is it in harmony with the stage of development of the nervous system? Does it preserve the freshness of intellectual attack? Are the children thoroughly interested? Are they sincere—that is, do they *desire* to do the work in hand? Are they unself-conscious, or are they thinking of what the teacher expects of them? Do they attack the work with joy and do they experience inner satisfaction and consciousness of power in doing it? The answers to these questions were not easy to find.

I had no expert criticism—no one to whom to turn for advice. I was trying to put into practical application the principles expressed in Oppenheim, Mondereon, Dewey and others. Whether knowledge and skill, which still seemed to me desirable, would be an inevitable accompaniment of a normal process of growth, remained to be seen.

What is normal growth? This question has never been answered, but even though we may never be able to find the correct answer, it is still our duty and privilege to try to provide right conditions for normal growth. I believe that this is the only defensible reason for the existence of schools.

Some of the mothers offered to pay a little tuition, but since I could not charge enough to support the school, I determined to keep it free to the local children. As a public school teacher, I had always felt rather superior to private schools, often accusing them of using "soft" pedagogy and having no standards. I determined that no child should ever be barred from the school for financial reasons. It was the greatest joy of my life just to have the privilege of trying out a theory which I felt to be so absolutely sound: *that education is life and that the school program, to be educational, must be life-giving!*

Parents and Teachers at School Function

2   MANAGING THE PARENTS

I have the greatest sympathy for the skeptical parent. He listens to the theory that education is growth and usually agrees heartily, but when he puts his child in school, he wants to be *shown*. He is afraid that the desired amount of "subject matter" will not be acquired. To think of growth in other terms than reading, writing, arithmetic, science, history, and geography is impossible for him. This idea harks back to the time when children did all work at home and the school was devoted solely to the acquisition of literacy.

We are all so materialistic! We want immediate, external, measurable results! Why should we subject the mind to measurement, when we never think of calling a child a failure because of height or weight, color of hair or eyes, nor do we standardize the emotions. A child is no more responsible for his interests and mental ability than for his physical characteristics. A modern school tried out the idea of allowing the children to grade each other's social qualities. One little girl struggling to evaluate her companion said, "Mother, I am going to give Sadie a 'C' in generosity, and I am going to give myself an 'A'. You know, Mother, I am more generous than Sadie." Many modern educators still insist that there shall be some measure, though not yet certain as to what it should be! Some of the stories of the Great Master should convince us that the elusive thing called *life* cannot be measured! Since life— growth—education—are synonymous, why try to measure education? This is no doubt due to our general commercialization. Since money is the false measure of industry, we have fallen into the error of rating *growth* by the acquisition of facts—the attainment of skills.

Increase in mental grasp, joy and interest, and physical vigor are often too imperceptible to be recognized readily and sometimes when these signs are quite apparent we fail to value them sufficiently. Some parents balked absolutely at the thought of not teaching their children to read and write until eight or nine years of age. "Will my child be ready, will he be 'up' with other children at ten, if he does not learn to read at six?" was the constant question, and the answer always, "I do not know, but he should not read now." Formal work should be postponed until at least ten years of age, but the parents' protest was so overpowering that we introduced this work at eight, though no particular standard is required. The teacher uses the best method she knows, her aim being to have the children enjoy learning to read—and when they love to do it, they do their best and that is enough.

The school process cannot be a "do as you please" affair because of the nature of childhood. Children have no basis for judgement, they do not know what is good for them, and their desires are often quite unwholesome. Sometimes children are perverted as well as some adults! Even though parents may agree that the child must be controlled and guided for his own good, they often insist that children should be allowed to read at an early age if they *want* to! If parents and teachers understood the order of the development of the nervous system, and the danger of the specialization required in learning to read, they could not be persuaded to allow such work.

"I cannot keep my child from reading," exclaims the proud Mother. "But," explains the teacher, "you keep him from doing other unwholesome things, why not direct his attention away from books until you are sure such work is desirable?" We are all so *personal*. We want our children to be unusual!! In one case where a mother insisted that her child was ready for reading and desired it, the teacher queried, "Are you sure that *he* wants to read, or do *you* want him to?" The mother insisted that the child wished to read. The teacher finally relented, saying, "Very well, if your child wishes to read, I will help him do so." After a few sincere efforts, the teacher discovered that the child was not really interested in learning to read, but had been stimulated by the mother until he thought he *ought* to want to. At the next interview with the mother, the teacher explained that the child did not care for reading and if he were really going to learn, pressure would have to be used. The mother exclaimed, "He doesn't want to read? Well, he will." And the next day, sure enough, the child showed quite a desire to read. Evidently, the mother had used pressure.

"My child is very intelligent. She knows more and has more power than any other child of seven," explains an ambitious father. "I am sure she is perfectly able to do the work of the eight- and nine-year-old children." "But," explained the teacher, "there is no special *work* that eight- and nine-year-old children must do. We merely provide the opportunities which seem appropriate for the group, giving special attention to the individual whenever necessary. Your child may need broadening by going more slowly and may be somewhat one-sidedly intellectual." So, we placed the seven-year-old child in her age group, giving her much more hand-work and free play, since she had already learned to read. The father felt that she was "marking time." In a few months, however, he came to us saying that he found his little girl was sleeping better, was much happier with her younger brothers and sisters, and that she seemed much more poised and less fretful and nervous than she had been. These human results are always there if we only were able to recognize them. Acceleration is not only bad for the nervous system, but when children are grouped with older children, problems of sex and social consciousness often develop a little later. Some of the most unhappy experiences we have had throughout the years have been with children and young people who have been accelerated! Such children are constantly bidding for adult attention, are often very changeable and capricious, and difficult in both work and play.

An eleven-year-old child was so conscious of her superiority that she was unable to make friends and became bitter and unhappy, becoming not only a behavior problem herself but interfering with the progress of her group. By placing her in her age group, making no demands of her either at home or at school, she improved tremendously, but may never fully overcome the ill effects of wrong conditions during childhood. A lengthening childhood, as society increases in complexity, is absolutely essential to progress. Everyone should read *The Meaning of Infancy* by

John Fiske if he would understand how necessary the prolonging of childhood is to the development of the race. Lack of poise, self-control, power of concentration, purposefulness, and inability to adjust socially are the most striking evidences of one-sided development. A thirteen-year-old child, ready for the third year of high school, was persuaded to enter her age group—eighth grade. Her mother was delighted at her progress and the child herself testified that she had learned more than ever even though she "had all that work before." One of the fallacies of our graded educational system is the idea that a student must have studied or mastered the work of all previous grades before entering upon that of the present grade. "Having had the work" of the previous grade is not so important as interest, desire, and mental grasp.

The little child should have much time for play and even for dreaming. If one may not dream in childhood, when will time be found for this accomplishment? Froebel said that many life situations are often worked out in childish play, and also that there are nerve processes that require absolute quiet, and that breaking into a child's apparent idle dreaming may interfere with growth.

The children were very fond of watching certain trees in the woods, claiming them, caring for them, and preventing mutilation by tourists. In discussing this with a mother who had put her child in another school so that she might "learn something," the mother said, "Oh yes, I know they enjoy that, but I'd rather my child were learning arithmetic than to be fooling with trees." "But," replied the teacher, "unless they have these intelligent experiences now when they are really interested, they may never acquire a love for trees —and we think it is the right of every child to have an opportunity to develop this love."

To have happy, interesting experiences with animals is much more educative to children than lessons about them.

Sometimes the mothers were quite horrified at seeing a
little girl calmly lift a huge live snake out of her blouse—but
all fear of snakes is overcome when children study and
handle them as pets. Children really love *nature* and it is
their *right* to have experiences which strengthen that love
and increase appreciation. A visitor taking a walk with the
children remarked about the keen, intelligent observation.
"I never walked with children who were so happily interested in things to see!" To recognize a rabbit track—to
note the hiding places of animals—and to be able to
understand the blossoming of the forest in the spring and
the preparation of all life for winter, is very thrilling.

A little girl came weeping to her teacher one day, saying,
"I must stay out of school. I must help father pick up sweet
potatoes. I may be absent two or three weeks." Well, replied
the teacher, "how nice it is that your father had a girl big
enough to help him." "Oh," said the child, "I will lose my
class." "No," said the teacher, "you cannot lose your class,
your class will be here when you come back." "Yes," said the
little girl, "but I will lose the work, I will get behind!" "Well,"
said the teacher, "you will lose a little of the school
work—true enough—but you will be learning how to take
care of sweet potatoes, and that is very important, you
know." So, the little girl stayed at home helping her father
and when she returned the teacher asked her to tell the
children all about the process of gathering and storing
sweet potatoes. This was most educational. The children
incidentally learned a great deal about moisture and its
effect on the potatoes, and the necessity for ventilation in
the storing. It was a great shock, however, to parents for the
school to substitute picking up sweet potatoes for school
work! In an economic system based upon the injustice of
monopoly, it is cruel indeed to punish children because of
their parents' inability to prosper under unjust conditions.
The school work should be so arranged that no child may

"get behind." The teacher should be free to substitute any wholesome activity for the school work. If education is *life, life* is also education. The schools place too great an emphasis upon lessons and the directed work of the school, and are altogether too indifferent to the home and out-of-school experiences which are often profoundly educational.

A father removed his child from the school, exclaiming in disgust, "They ask my child how *old* she is. They never find out how much she knows!" But another father brought his children to the school, saying, "My children do not know how to play. I want them to be real children." Sometime we are going to recognize free play, initiative, and social adjustments as *real* "subject matter."

Thirty years ago this point of view was so new that many people felt it was dangerous and that the school should not be allowed to continue. Every possible criticism was made and in some places these criticisms are, no doubt, continuing to be made of any innovation in the school program. One popular criticism was that the children were allowed to do as they pleased too much. In spite of the fact that I make a point of explaining that it is *not* a "do as you please" process, people continue to assume that it is!

Often parents complained that the children were not learning anything. Others thought the work of the school was too casual. If education is growth, we are obliged to respect the inner movement of growth. Children languish when subjected to constant direction. The child suffers from fatigue more quickly under direction than in any other way. When interesting work furnishes direction, there is joy and enthusiasm and little or no danger of fatigue. When schools are wise enough to provide the finest discipline through creative activity, parents will not desire the discipline of personal authority. The old quarrel between the advocates of the theory of interest and that of

discipline must cease as soon as people realize that interest
and discipline are connected, not opposed.

One gentleman explained that when he was a boy he
disliked going to school, but found out that he had no
choice in the matter. He insisted that it is normal for
children to hate school and that when they love to go there
must be something vitally wrong with the school! We have
yet to learn that one may be as truly disciplined by pleasant
activity as by performing disagreeable tasks.

One little boy did not learn to read, write, or spell readily,
so his father put him in the public school. Later, when he
was in his "teens" and ready for high school, he still could
not read or spell well. The father then frankly admitted that
if this condition were found in the Experimental School, he
would have blamed the school, but since the child had been
in public school, the father felt that something must be
wrong with the boy! Parents often contend that certain
children need to be held to intellectual tasks with severity.
They do not trust interest or the processes of growth. One
often hears these children exclaiming, "Oh, I don't care
how well I do the work, as long as I barely pass." We cannot
overestimate the loss to individual power caused by this
fundamental insincerity. The unconventional school is
always judged severely if "results" are not apparent, but
when undesirable results occur in the conventional school,
the child is blamed.

"Are you going to teach them manners?" "Don't you
think a child should be taught to behave?" inquires an
anxious mother. But manners are the result of the atmosphere in which the child lives and largely due to the
patterns he sees. The gentle mother does not usually have
an ill-mannered child, unless she has pampered and spoiled
the child. Of course, children are uncontrolled and impul-
sive, but if the spirit is sweet and sincere and if they love
their work, the proper relation to others will develop,

especially if they are treated with consideration by teachers and parents, and are allowed free association with others in work and play. Since love is the law, isn't it strange that adults do not give more attention to the emotional life of children in connection with intellectual activity? Why should we care so much more for what children *learn* and *can* do than for what they enjoy and love? I do not mean that there shall be *no* correction of ill behavior. Every case of wrong action should be dealt with on its merits, but we find much less quarreling and much more happiness and good will where there is no competition in the work; and where the children do not feel the pressure of external standards, they are less nervous and irritable. The all-important art of human relations cannot be acquired unless children are allowed the fullest opportunity to humanly relate! This cannot be accomplished when the school day is given over to the assignment of tasks and the hearing of lessons! *Children should not be conscious of adult expectancy. This is a source of self-consciousness and waste in childhood.*

Parents are often sensitive about their children's accomplishments and feel humiliated if they do not compare favorably with others. "My boy's little cousin can write letters to his friends, but my boy cannot. He often feels very much ashamed and the other children make fun of him because he cannot read or write." The parent may easily protect the child by letting him feel that the many other things he *can* do are more important and interesting than reading and writing. If parents had a deep *conviction* in the matter—if they felt certain that the formal work *should* be postponed—there would be very little or no complaint from the children! The fear that children will be unable to enter certain grades in the conventional schools is a real obstacle. Removing all entrance requirements would remedy this. The idea that education is a *preparation* for something in the future has such a strong hold upon the

imagination that few parents can believe that if the need of
the present is met fully, the future is assured. Growth has
no external end. The end and the process are one. If the
child is happily engaged in wholesome activity, he is
growing, he is being educated.

After many years of experience in this work, we find that
the child who would normally be promoted in the conventional school is usually accepted in the grade of his years on
leaving our school, even though he may not have had the
particular work of that grade, and very often the children
from our school have been graded beyond their years on
entering other schools. Frequently, the report has come
back that the children are unusually strong, keenly interested, and self-reliant.

A child came running into the school one day, exclaiming, "Oh, Miss L, there are snakes under the house!"
Without a moment's hesitation the teacher and every child
in the room went out to see the snakes. The teacher felt this
was more important than to make them wait until the close
of the session. But some of the parents complained that
there was no "discipline." The conventional educational
process is too fixed—too conscious—too external. Dewey
says we should always keep in mind that no knowledge or
discipline is of value unless it is immediately important.

A man drove into town with an alligator on his wagon. It
was an enormous creature, occupying the whole wagon and
extending some distance beyond. It was dead. Of course, all
the children had to go to see it, and the rest of the day was
spent in discussion. Some parents thought the school work,
thus omitted, should be made up. We have always been
happy to say that we never make up work in the elementary
school.

Each day's activity is important and enough in itself. Shall
we ever realize that learning is a result of experience, not
merely acquiring facts? Why should we think that the

teacher and children must always be conscious of some specific ordered task of learning—why not trust the natural movement of mind in interested activity?

Sometimes we have been accused of having little or no organization. Much initiative has been lost, many fine aspirations have been destroyed, by too much organization. The aim is all-round development and the school should always be willing to allow children to use their intelligence in meeting novel situations. Children do not thrive in institutions. Life—growth—cannot be forced into patterns! An institution is of value only as it serves, never when it controls. How much happier and freer—yes, and how much more would be learned—if teacher and pupil were free from the demands of a curriculum!

The wise teacher always takes advantage of the moments when desire is strong and interest keen. "The source of power is in the emotions." Still, we do have a daily program which is followed, though it is always subject to change without notice.

Some parents bring their backward children to the Experimental School and expect the school to make geniuses of them. They are not satisfied that the child now holds his head up, that he is becoming unself-conscious, that he is eager for his work, that he uses his intelligence to the highest advantage, that he is happy and sincere; they feel that he must rank in information and skill with the more gifted children. Every child should be given the best opportunity to develop as far and in as fine a way as possible for *him*.

A little boy made a beautiful tray of clay, but when urged to make another, he was unable to do so. He had become self-conscious by the attention given. Children's work should not be compared with that of others. If we could only learn that every human being is a unique individual, making demands that we must meet, we should not so often be guilty of comparing one child with another—either in work or behavior. We often see work posted for observation of visitors. The names and often the ages of the children are given. This develops self-consciousness. The name and age should always be omitted.

It takes a long time for fathers and mothers to realize that children's work is naturally imperfect and unfinished and that they should not always be obliged to finish everything that they begin. I am always rather skeptical about exhibits. Even when the work is genuinely children's work, the exhibit does now show what that work did to the children! It is true children should be given work which will sustain interest and should be helped persevere, but the young child is undeveloped and should not be held to any degree of perfection. Sometimes the pasting of pictures by children in the kindergarten is very neat. This always suggests the hand of the teacher—or, too severe guidance. Children's work is always sloppy, unfinished, imperfect. If we are going to administer to growth, we must give time for growth. The question in the mind of the teacher should always be, "What effect is the work having on the children?"—not "How excellent is it?"

Right here I want to plead for more free time for children—both at home and at school and in summer camps! A little boy complained, "I never have time to do what I want to do!" Too often, the elders feel that the children's time must be fully "occupied" and supervised! The adult then plans activities for the children from the moment of rising until retiring. This is too strenuous for the adult and very bad—yes, weakening—for the children. Complaints may be made that there is not enough to do, that the children are bored, etc., but persistence in a program allowing long spaces of undirected activity always results in the development of initiative, poise, and resourcefulness.

"My boy does nothing but play," complained one father. It is true his boy was the captain of the team and was a wonderful baseball player—but he did his academic work with almost the same zest that he showed on the playground. The father, however, was not satisfied with that; he saw the child at play and heard him discussing the play, and felt that this was quite out of harmony with the serious business of school.

Few parents and teachers realize the great educational value of play. The poise, coordination, intellectual power and social qualities developed in play are of inestimable human value. Play is the most important educational experience. All creative hand-work might justly be classified as play. The greatest minds are those able to use the play spirit in their work. Routine and external pressure are the cause of many a nervous break—many a failure among adults.

The Doctor announced one day that he had advised Mary's mother to take her out of school. "Why is that?" asked the teacher. "The child is not well," replied the doctor, "and can not sit still in school." "But, she doesn't have to sit still in school," the teacher insisted. "Well," said the doctor, "she cannot go on those long walks that the children take." The teacher replied, "She need not take the long walks." "Well, she should stay at home and play with her dolls," exclaimed the doctor. "But she may bring her dolls to school," insisted the teacher. "Isn't there anything in the school that the child *has* to do?" The doctor questioned. The teacher replied, "The school demands nothing which you and the child's mother and the teacher think is unwise for her." "Hmm," said the doctor, "I didn't know you were running a sanitorium." "That is just what we are doing!" exclaimed the teacher. "We are trying to eliminate everything from our school which could possibly militate against the all-round health of the child, and we are

trying to include everything in the school which will make
for a fine body, an intelligent mind, and a sweet spirit."
  The strangest thing of all, in dealing with parents, is to
find some who accept the theory fully, insisting that they
want just such a school for their children—that it is what
they have long been looking for—and the moment their
children are entered, begin to try to change the whole aim
and practice of the school! "I want my child to do this work
in arithmetic so that he may go on with his group in the
home school," or "I know my child is ready and can do the
work of a higher grade!" Only once or twice in all the years
have I found parents requesting that their children be
grouped with those slightly younger. Such parents often
refuse to allow the school to decide upon the group the
children shall enter. A mother insists upon her child of
twelve joining an adult group, although a children's class is
available.
  One mother exclaimed, "I am very particular that my
children are given the strongest mental stimulus," And the
children were living proofs of the error! They were
nervous, self-conscious, and quite unsocial. Parents often
demand that *their* children be taught things not offered by
the school, even though this requires much extra time of
the teacher. The usual reason given is that the child may not
remain in this school long and he must be ready for the
school he will attend later.
  Our graded, marking school system is responsible for a
vast amount of misunderstanding and misdirecting—yes,
and misery of children. Sometimes the parent wishes his
child to "skip a grade," often insisting that he is "bored" by
the "baby work" of his age group. The bored child is usually
one who has been over-stimulated and made too conscious
of *learning!*
  A ten-year-old child constantly trying to attract the
attention of adults—showing her accomplishments, taking

part in adult conversation, avoiding companionship with children of her age—is an accelerated, languishing child, even though her mother thinks her marvelous! A child of seven is not happy creating many interesting things with the seven-year-old children—but is taken out of school because she wants to work with older groups. Organic education does not mean that children shall "do as they please." It means that the adult shall insist upon the child doing that which is wholesome for him. If this mother had allowed her child to remain in school, encouraging her to enter into the seven-year-old activities, no doubt real improvement in the child's growth would soon have been apparent.

Many young people have come to us who are pathetic results of over-stimulation! A young man half through college at eighteen came to us to recuperate—rest—engage in creative art work, and if possible, escape "dementia praecox." He escaped. A young woman wishing to become a teacher, but too delicate physically—worn out getting her M.D. and Ph.D.! No doubt all the progressive schools have had similar experiences—young people, unsocial, lacking in human power, but who have diplomas and degrees, having met the academic requirements of the "system." The time will come when people will not have to *earn* a degree! The "system" will change its point of view. Then people will study because they want to know, and joy of knowing will be the only reward!

We have always grouped our children according to their chronological age. This, we believe, prevents self-consciousness. The precocious child may be given more work without being forced into the sex and social consciousness of older children; the backward child may work along at his own pace without being prodded or humiliated by odious comparisons or markings. Even though he may need some special assistance at times, it is never given with the idea of "keeping up" with the class. The children merely spend a

year engaged in wholesome, happy, interesting occupations adapted to that stage of development, engaging in
more advanced work as they are able.

It has always been a very comfortable thing for our school
to have a very excellent public school in town to which
parents may send their children if they are not satisfied with
what our school is doing. No mother will ever admit that she
is forcing her child. "No, indeed, I wouldn't have my child
pushed, but he is marking time or really doing *nothing* in the
group of his age." "He needs to be made to *concentrate*. I was
always at the top of the class in school and I am sure my
child is also going to be. His father is a college man and I am
a college woman!" Of course, the inference is that he has an
unusual mentality and that, therefore, he should be with
older children. In the long run, however, after all these
struggles, we have abundant testimony from parents that
the plan of having them work in their age group is perhaps
the better way. Since there must be some basis for grouping,
we believe the easier, simpler, more just plan is that of
chronological age.

Some parents have employed tutors to teach their
children reading and writing at home. When they insist that
the child *wants* to read and that, therefore, he should read,
we reply that our school is not a "do as you please" school,
that children must do as they are told; but we are under
obligations to provide for them the thing that we feel is
really good for them, and from our study of the development of the child, we think they should not be put at books
until the ninth or tenth year.

Some parents have brought their children to our school
because the burden of lessons and assigned tasks in the
conventional school has been too heavy for them. Usually
such children have blossomed perceptibly in a short time.
Many children have come to us in a nervous, run-down
condition, and in a few weeks have almost, if not fully,

recovered. And sometimes parents put their children with us until they are "strong enough" to endure the pressure of the regular school!

We believe that when external pressure is removed, there is an inner movement which must eventually take place and this should be nourished and vitalized. Very often children who are behavior problems have seemed to outgrow these difficulties. This is largely due to a sense of freedom and unself-consciousness developed by the school. Sometimes the children themselves, no doubt stimulated by their parents, say they are not learning anything, but on second thought they often say, "Well, I think we are learning just as much, perhaps even more than we did in the other school, but we don't *know* that we are!"

Eventually, adults will prize the signs of healthy growth in children. Spontaneity, initiative, interest, mental grasp, sincerity, and unself-consciousness will be counted more desirable than mere attainment and achievement, and this will be a splendid foundation for learning, when the natural unfoldment and gradual strengthening of the mind is ready for the more exacting and sustained academic work of later years.

Extensive Travel Required

3   FINDING SUPPORT

But how could the school be financed? The twenty-five dollars per month offered in the beginning put the school through the first year. The fact that I had been a training teacher in a Teachers' College induced a young woman wishing to become a teacher to study with me, assisting with the children for practice.

The next year Mr. Joseph Fels visited Fairhope in the interests of the Single Tax.* He became interested in what looked to him like a play school, and made inquiries about

---

*The Single Tax concept of land usage and ownership is discussed at length in *Progress and Poverty,* by Henry George, Walter J. Black, Inc., New York, N.Y., 1942; and in *Fairhope,* by Paul E. and Blanche R. Alyea, The University of Alabama Press, 1956, reprinted 1973. (ed. note)

the principles upon which we were working. He gave the school one thousand dollars. The school was now moved from my own cottage into a small building, and an assistant was engaged. The enrollment reached about thirty-five. Mr. Fels again gave the school a gift of five thousand dollars and promised one thousand dollars a year for a period of five years. With this fund to administer, the school was incorporated, and then we acquired the present site of about ten acres, with a main school building of three large rooms.

Other rooms have been added from year to year, until at the present time (1938) there are on the campus: a building containing two rooms for the kindergarten and "first life" class, another two-room building for class room and science laboratory, a shop of three rooms, the high school building, a cottage for music and one for English, a hall for dramatics, basketball, parties, etc., a dormitory for boarding pupils, a recreation room, beside the original building of three rooms. All buildings should be repaired or replaced. More class rooms are needed, the shop should be enlarged, and a library and new dormitory are pressing for realization.

But one thousand dollars a year was not enough to support the school, and so the raising of funds was added to my duties. Throughout all the years, Mrs. Lydia J. Comings of Fairhope has devoted an unswerving interest to this work, being business manager and President of the Board until her health forced her to relinquish the management, though still retaining membership on the Board.

A friend in the North, hearing the story of the school and its needs, said that to support this work would require the writing of an infinite number of letters, and advised that I never grow discouraged but continue writing and asking.

This I have done and still continue to solicit help, and even after all the years some friends continue their contributions. Many have been reduced, but the wonder is that

they continue at all! This advice has been a source of
strength to me, helping through many dark hours. We have
never known at the opening of school in September that the
work would really continue until June, and still the teachers
have dared to accept positions, and during the last distressing times have agreed to continue to work with the
understanding that in case the school is unable to pay the
amount agreed upon, there would be no indebtedness
hanging over the organization!! Perhaps that is why the
school still carries on!

Once when the way seemed particularly dark, a friend
admonished: "You know this work should be done. If you
do not do it, who will?" My experience as a money raiser has
been very thrilling and most interesting. While there have
been many times when discouragement and despair
seemed to brood over me, I have been able to come through
and have now a greater faith in mankind than ever. Instead
of thinking how selfish and mean people are, one should
rejoice that they are as kind and cooperative as one finds
them. And people are really very kind. I know I became a
real nuisance and annoyance to many, and blamed only
myself when eager hopes were dashed by a cool rejection of
my plea.

A small incidental fee was charged for supplies and use of
books, but the main support of the school had to be secured
from interested friends. Children from a distance pay a
nominal tuition and a boarding department became a great
help, but when Mr. Fels' bequest was exhausted the need
for contributions was greatly increased. I usually spent the
entire day at school, then after my housework was finished I
continued—sometimes far into the night—writing letters to
secure support. I have never been able to commercialize the
work—have never been able to develop it into an income-
bearing project. The suggestion has been made that we
launch a publicity campaign and thus secure support, but

we have never had anything to sell and have always been so grateful for the privilege of working in so great a cause, we could not advertise.

The *idea* that education is growth and that the school program must minister to growth so fully possessed me that I have always been most grateful for the privilege of working at it. I have been condemned for not "building up" a supporting organization. My only defense is that we have had to work so hard for the immediate necessity, we have had no time or strength to give to planning for the future. There has never been an endowment nor even a promised support covering a number of years. We have literally lived from hand to mouth.

Once I was invited to address a meeting of a Mothers' Congress in Pennsylvania. At that time, I traveled usually in the day coach in the daytime and sometimes at night, and I often traveled the whole distance from Mobile to New York without entering the diner; sometimes taking a lunch, but often fasting. I have always felt that it is a wholesome thing for adults to fast occasionally. It gives one such a conscious-ness of strength to refrain from eating on principle rather than because of an empty pocketbook!

Just as the train was leaving Mobile, I discovered, to my horror, that I had failed to supply my purse with change. I had my ticket as far as Washington, but the wherewithal to continue my journey to Williamsport was not in evidence. In my despair, I tried to induce the Pullman conductor to cash a check for me. He politely declined. The next morning at Chattanooga, I tried another conductor. He likewise declined, but suggested that I telegraph back to my bank asking that the money be sent to me at Bristol. At Bristol there was no sign of money. We were reaching Washington the next morning. How to get to Williamsport was my problem. I finally gained courage enough to lay my troubles before a friendly looking gentleman across the aisle. He asked a few questions and I told him frankly that I had failed to get cash in Mobile and was now penniless on the way to Williamsport. He said he would cash a check for me. The next morning I offered to give him the check, but he replied that he was going in that direction and would buy my ticket to Williamsport. He then invited me to have breakfast with him. I demurred at first, but finally accepted and became acquainted with one of the most kindhearted and sincerest businessmen it has ever been my privilege to meet. He was much interested in the spirit of cooperation in business. He made me believe for the first time in my life that it is possible for a businessman to be a Christian. He asked about the school and I told him the principles upon which we were working. He became deeply interested in the idea and cooperated in every way possible for as long as he lived. The life of the school has many times been saved at critical moments through his help. The school has never had a more true-hearted, interested friend than the late Mr. W. J. Hoggson of Greenwich and New York.

As we neared his destination, I was again overwhelmed with humiliation because, while he had bought my ticket, I had no cash in my purse and would require street-car fare to get to the place of meeting. In great confusion, I told him my predicament and asked to borrow a nickel! He offered a ten-dollar bill for the cause. As it happened, my place of meeting was in the yard of the station at Williamsport, so I was able to send the ten dollars to our treasurer in Fairhope, asking her to write a letter of acknowledgment at once to the donor.

I was invited to speak at a meeting of the Home and School Association in Philadelphia soon after this. I tried in ten minutes to explain what we think are the fundamentals of moral training. I explained that if children are provided with exercises and activities that are in harmony with their stage of development, that meet the needs of growth, that satisfy desire, they *are sincere* and unself-conscious, and that the only reward is inner satisfaction and consciousness of power, and that this is the fundamental of all moral character! I explained that the grading, marking system causes self-consciousness and often develops insincerity, which is fundamental immorality! Mrs. Woodrow Wilson and other distinguished people were at the meeting and expressed full agreement with the principles of morality for which I contended. The response from the audience was electrical; there were two encores, reporters crowded about after the meeting, and many appointments to speak in and about Philadelphia followed. And, of course, all of this resulted in more or less financial help for the school.

I finally found my way to New York City and told Mr. Hoggson of the reception which the idea was receiving. He at once made an appointment for me to speak in Greenwich at his home. At this meeting I met Mrs. Charles D. Lanier, who has been one of my warmest friends ever since and always one of the strongest supporters of the idea. While Mrs. Lanier was unable to contribute large sums of money to the cause, her work in countless other ways resulted in perhaps greater support for the idea than great financial contributions could have done.

A summer school was immediately planned and I went up from Fairhope for a six weeks' course in Greenwich, Connecticut, in the summer of 1913. Nineteen or twenty adult students attended this first summer school. The program consisted of one period devoted to the study of childhood, a storytelling hour, folk dancing and hand-work, and two hours in the morning were devoted to working with the children. The summer school was conducted in a public school building, no tuition was charged, and nearly one hundred public school children came in. All of the adults became student teachers during the morning session. It was a real revelation to many to see children

joyously attending summer school without thought of
credit, making up work, or pressure of any kind! Children
love to learn! The mind wants knowledge as the stomach
wants food!

At this summer school, a conference was held and the
matter of support for the Fairhope School was considered.
A Fairhope League was organized, with Mrs. Lanier as
President and Mr. W. J. Hoggson, Treasurer. An appeal
was made for contributions and enough money was raised
to carry the school through another year. Then the
Secretary, Miss Jean L. Hunt, did valiant service for several
years, making speaking appointments, arranging for summer schools, and promoting the idea in every possible way.
The Fairhope Summer School, sponsored by the Fairhope
League, became a Northern extension of the Fairhope
School. While it did not contribute to the immediate
financial support of the school, it helped to extend the idea
and secured friends and thus became a great asset.

In 1921 a special Winter School for fathers, mothers,
teachers, social workers, and children was offered at
Fairhope for six weeks in February and March. This has
been of some financial help to the school.

John Dewey, of Columbia University, was invited to come
to Fairhope and investigate the school. He came during the
Christmas vacation and the school remained in session for
his visit. He spent a great deal of time in the shop. In
response to a question about the manual training, he
replied, "It is good. On the whole, it is the best I have ever
seen. Usually, when the children are free, the technique is
not good, and when the technique is good the children are
not free. Here, the technique is good and the children are
free." He also commented upon the adaptation of means to
ends which he characterized as "intellectual sincerity." The
thought of being "investigated" and the fear that his report
might be unfavorable constituted the most critical experi-

ence of my life! My little Son comforted me by exclaiming, "Of course the report will be favorable, because it can't be anything else!"

John Dewey's report of the work has been of inestimable value, not only in establishing it in the minds of educators and others, but it has been a tremendous help in securing funds. His report has had the greatest influence in securing the favorable attention of educators in the South. While the school has not received financial aid from the South, nearly all of the educational institutions have been friendly and sympathetic. This spirit of friendly interest is growing.

Then I was invited to direct Mrs. Lanier's little school in Greenwich, which made it possible for me to continue my work in the Fairhope School without compensation. I received a small salary from the Northern school and supplemented it by part of my lecture fees. Since the lecture work developed through an effort to spread the idea and find support for the school, the greater portion of the fees belonged to the Cause.

This conducting to two schools so far apart was fraught with many difficulties and abundant criticism was offered, but this enabled me to go North and gave me an opportunity to see people of means and so solicit funds for the school at Fairhope.

I have spent many hours at the telephone booth trying to make appointments, hoping to get help. Many people could not see that education needed to change its *direction*. The external standard seemed natural and desirable. Many insisted that childen should be rewarded for study and could not see that study is its own reward and that other rewards develop double motives and fundamental insincerity. Some people were quite conscious of the fact that children do not always thrive physically in school; that they do often become nearsighted, round-shouldered, and nervous; but they saw no way to change the work.

At a large educational conference, a speaker exhibited a photograph of twelve hundred children wearing glasses! This, he insisted was necessary to avoid eye strain. No one even hinted that the work might be changed to escape eye strain! I am very sure that the idea of preserving sincerity and consequent morality through happy, unself-conscious activity, without the undermining influence of the double or false motives of grades and marks, seemed to many people most visionary and impractical. The idea that direct conscious moral training is necessary is still quite prevalent. Many plans and schemes were presented for moral training. Usually they are lessons *about* morals, but the idea that conditions might be changed so that children unconsciously live sincerely and so establish a moral basis, is still to be accepted! We are guilty of subjecting children to a process developing insincerity, and then we give lessons in morals!

At an educational conference an official was instructing teachers in methods of moral and health education. When someone asked, "Would it not be well to try to eliminate from the school program those features which may be inimical to health and morals, such as marks and grades, which develop double motives, and severe forms of specialized activity, which may impair the nervous system?" the instructor exclaimed. "Oh, we don't want to go into that."

Sometimes generous contributions were given; occasionally they were refused with considerable firmness and utter lack of interest, and sometimes they were refused with regret. However, in the main, I have found people of great means very willing to listen to the story of an obscure school many miles away, which was making an effort to work out an ideal. It might have been easier if the appeal had been for crippled children, or for children in homes of hopeless poverty, but to appeal for help to work out a new *standard* in education, was too great an innovation and too uncertain to receive ready or unqualified approval. One gentleman said, "Your appeal is not for tubercular nor paralyzed children, not neglected news-boys, nor abandoned babies nor fallen girls. These have a direct human appeal. Your cause will bless all children in the present and in the future and therefore you may expect scant attention and response." The fact that a new standard was contemplated seemed to discredit the present school system, which some resented. "Did you attend the public schools?" When the answer was given in the affirmative, the retort was, "You are repudiating the process that made you, isn't that base ingratitude?" To which the only response is, "I am grateful for every good that ever came to me, but perhaps if my elders had understood the nature and needs of childhood, I might have escaped many limitations."

Very few people are able to work for a cause, the results of which will bless children yet unborn! We are all still inclined to be too personal. This, no doubt, is largely due to the educational process through which we have passed. It tends to develop a self-consciousness which prevents un-prejudiced thinking. This is a form of arrest of development which seems to be well-nigh universal. Economic reformers cannot understand the inability of the man in the street to recognize the fundamental injustice of our monopolistic economic order. If sincerity and openness of mind could be preserved in every school by eliminating external standards, no doubt human progress would be much more rapid and certain. But now we often hear parents exclaim, "I came through the educational system —look at me." The retort, of course, is, "Perhaps that is the cause of your shortcomings."

I have had help at unexpected moments. Once I needed one thousand dollars to finish the school year. I secured an interview with a woman of means and when the situation was explained, she said, "Well, let's write out a check at

once!" and proceeded to give me one thousand dollars! My
joy knew no bounds and I have blessed her ever since. One
friend financed one of our high school graduates through
college. "This is one of the ways to prove your work
successful," she said. Refusals have not embittered me and I
have only the kindliest feelings toward those who have not
helped.

Once a very rich woman explained, "I am sorry, but I
cannot give anything for your work." In explaining the
refusal to a friend, he exclaimed, "She lies, for I know that
she is abundantly able!" But I accepted it without a
murmur, because in reality she could not help even though
she might have plenty of money, for she did not *see* that this
work was worthy.

I entered a very rich man's office in the fullest expectancy
of receiving a generous contribution. He listened to my
story politely. Suddenly he put his finger on a button and
the door opened. With a wave of his hand, he said, "Give
her twenty-five dollars." Quite a shock to one's nervous
system when expecting something like twenty-five
thousand dollars! Some people hesitated because they did
not know that the school was incorporated and thought the
cause too personal. On hearing, however, that it is a
responsible institution, they often still failed to assist!

After I directed Mrs. Lanier's school for two years, she
turned it over to me, and changing its name and location,
we proceeded to make of it a center in the North for
demonstrating the Fairhope idea. The principles on which
we are working are not new, nor original. They have been
expressed again and again, and repeated efforts have been
made to apply them practically. But each application does
become an original demonstration. This idea expressed by
such authorities as Nathan Oppenheim, C. Manford Henderson, John Dewey, Froebel and others, is as universally
accepted as a theory as it is violated in practice. Some one
replied to my appeal. "History is strewn with such efforts as

yours." Our comfort is that it is a joy to work at so great an idea and that educational sentiment is changing! The fact that the efforts do not survive does not prove them of no value!

Very soon we found that even in the center of great wealth a school might struggle for its existence. We occupied a summer building for one year, but found it most inadequate. It could not be properly heated and there were no facilities for caring for the boarding pupils within comfortable distance. A beautiful residence had been partially burned and I set my heart upon securing that place for the school. Of course, to buy it was out of the question, but at least I thought we might borrow it. It was boarded up and was in the hands of a caretaker.

One morning I went to the owner's residence. The butler told me that she wasn't up. I asked when she would be up and he said in about an hour—and I assured him that I would return. In the meantime, I walked about the streets in New York and telephoned, asking for an interview. She consented to see me. Upon my return, the butler told me that she was out. I said that he must be mistaken since I had telephoned her and she was expecting me. I was then ushered into her presence.

Her first question was: "What do you want?" I replied, "I want your place at Greenwich." "What for?" she asked. "A school," I answered. She then asked, "Do you want me to *give* it to you?" "Yes", I answered. "Do you know," she cried, "that you are asking for three hundred and sixty thousand dollars worth of property?" "People have given more than that for an idea," was my reply.

I then explained briefly the aim of the school. She then said, "You could not use it if I should give it to you". "Why not?" I urged. "It will cost you forty thousand dollars to put it in condition." "Then," I replied, "we cannot use it, but isn't there a garage or something we can use?" "There are the stables," she replied. "You might use them. Go and look them over and if you can use them I shall be glad to let you have them for a couple of years." "Rent free?" I queried. "Certainly." I went out to Greenwich and went through the grounds—one of the show places in that beautiful town. "Come," said I to my friends, "the place is ours!" Isn't it beautiful—isn't it marvelous that we are to use this place and these grounds?" The house had been badly damaged by fire, but one wing was wholly untouched. This could be used for the boarding department, and the stables, with a few alterations, could easily be converted into classrooms. She gave us a two-year lease, which was afterwards renewed for one year. With the deepest gratitude and enthusiasm we entered upon the work of this Northern demonstration, telling her that we were determined to turn this place into a paradise for children.

The responsibility for two schools would have been overwhelming if it had not been for the untiring, devoted efforts of Mrs. C. D. Lanier. While she laid no claim to the school, her cooperation was as hearty as though it were still her personal project. It was the finest example of disinterested service, continued over many years, I have ever known. Some of my friends advised giving up the school at Fairhope and concentrating upon the Northern demonstration, but I could never feel quite willing to do this. The simple environment at Fairhope, the fact of charging no tuition from the people of the vicinity, gave a freedom to work out an idea which could not be approached in the more sophisticated community, though I hoped to be able to work out the principle in the more complex environment and fully believed this to be quite possible.

When the school at Greenwich passed into other hands, I still received no salary at Fairhope, depending on lecture fees for my personal support. My efforts in soliciting funds for the work were strengthened by the fact that I had no personal share in the budget.

I have never been able to have a stipulated lecture fee. I have always been glad to give my lectures for whatever the group is able and willing to pay—and this plan avoided a financial relation to my audience!

The Fairhope League became unable to pay its secretary, and for a number of years the funds were most uncertain, being largely secured by personal solicitation. An invitation came for me to speak in Detroit. In my audience were Mr. and Mrs. Henry Ford and their son Edsel and his wife. During the lecture, the fact was brought out that the school was in need of funds. After the lecture I met the Fords and they were most cordial. Mrs. Ford assured me that she heartily approved of the principles I had been advocating. I returned that I was delighted to hear this because I now felt certain she would help, and she answered that she would.

Then I asked if she would head a subscription. She replied in the affirmative, and when I asked her if she would make it large, she said she would make it as large as her husband, who was standing nearby, would permit. Then calling to him, she asked, "May I make a contribution to Mrs. Johnson's work?" He replied, "Yes, that's what I would like to have you do." Then I stepped up to him, asking him in a low tone, "May she make it large?" His reply was, "She may make it just as large as you can get her to make it." I then asked her for a million, but later received a check for twelve thousand dollars. Later, Mrs. Ford financed a lecture course for me in Detroit and Mr. and Mrs. Edsel Ford made contributions.

The response from people all over the country has been indeed marvelous!

We all wonder how the school has been preserved throughout the years! During the World War, a gentleman of great wealth replied, on being solicited for aid, "This is not the moment." I suppose it would be safe to say that donations from one dollar to thousands of dollars have come from people of little or no means to those of great wealth.

I have given "courses" in many cities and turned the fees in to the school treasury. The people of California as well as New York, and in cities between, have been most sympathetic and responsive.

The citizens of Fairhope have always been most friendly and cooperative. The town authorities have furnished the school with electricity and water without charge, and no taxes have been required from the beginning. Almost every year patrons of the school have furnished all the fuel for the school buildings. Many of the stores have given generous discounts and some have sold the school home, provisions at cost. The indebtedness on the school home was at one time raised by a public campaign. A large thermometer was placed in the center of the town and as contributions came in, a red line was extended until it reached the top and the entire debt was discharged.

Citizens and students have helped to construct and repair buildings. A group of mothers did the school laundry for two years as a contribution to the work. Entertainments, dances, sales, teas, suppers, etc., etc., have been constantly given for the benefit of the school. One woman has conducted a community luncheon for many years and has also sold refreshments at evening parties for the benefit of the school. Bread has been baked, and a number of the patrons canned vegetables and fruits, filling the school larder in the summer, enough to last throughout the year. A Thanksgiving shower is an annual affair. We were not always able to pay all bills at the close of school, and some merchants waited patiently all summer, often at great inconvenience to themselves.

Then we decided that unless we could pay bills at the close of school in June, we would not open in the fall. One year, the lack was so great the end seemed certain, when quite unexpectedly and without solicitation came a check which put us "over the top" for that year!

It would seem that such cooperation would almost if not fully support the school, but the children of the vicinity have never paid a tuition, only a $6.00 a year incidental fee. The school has supplied all books for the elementary school. The alumni association has cooperated, putting a roof on the school home and contributing other repairs. A friend of the school contributed a heating plant consisting of twin Arcolas and a full system of radiators, sending a man to install it. Another friend built a wading pool for the children of the kindergarten and contributed a radio. Dishes have been contributed as well as vegetables, canned goods, and other food stuffs. A printing press was contributed, and a friend of the school superintended the building of the shop and friendly architects contributed the plans. Gifts have been many and constant. Friends paid the salary for special teachers of music, dancing, and sewing.

A support of at least $20,000 per year for fifteen years should be found. The thirtieth Anniversary, which is approaching, is an appropriate time for this accomplishment.

The boarding department became an increasing source of support. At first, we placed the price for boarding pupils at five hundred dollars per year, then later at seven hundred and fifty—and finally reached one thousand dollars, but reduced it materially during these later years.

The boarding department is for boys and girls. This was unusual at that time and the growth has been very slow. It should be quite possible, eventually, to support the school through the boarding department and the tuition of day pupils coming from a distance, and still keep it free to the children of the vicinity.

If adequate support could be secured for a number of years, self-support would probably be accomplished in the not-distant future.

The school must become a permanent center of agitation and demonstration. In the measure that the school program meets the needs of the unfolding organism of the growing child, it is educational. All institutions of learning must eventually become educational!

Results of a Class Project

4 LITTLE CHILDREN

It is one thing to have an educational theory; it is something
quite different to put it into practice. The town of Fairhope
is an effort to make a "good theory work," so this is an
eminently appropriate location for a school working out a
good theory. The town of Fairhope is conducted on the
theory that community values belong to the community and
that values created by the individual belong to the individual. It is not so much interested to change the economic
capitalistic system as it is to establish justice, removing the
monopolistic feature. It believes that allowing individuals to
acquire the values belonging to the community and then
taxing the values created by the individual constitute two

very grave fundamental injustices, which are the basis of
many wrong economic conditions.

An old gentleman, after a lengthy discussion of our
educational theory, used to exclaim, "It is a splendid
theory; but it can't be done—I tell you, it can't be done!!"
The response to that is, "It is not a good theory if it will not
work." We may fail in its application, but the theory must be
practical or it is false!

The aim of the school is to study to know and meet the
needs of the growing organism; that is, to conduct a school
program which will preserve the sincerity and unself-
consciousness of the emotional life—provide for the finest,
keenest intellectual activity, and minister to the all-round
development of the nervous system. Ministering to growth,
meeting the needs of the organism, is the sole function of
the educational process—hence the term "organic." The
child is a reaching organism and the test of the environment
is his reaction. A bad child may not come from a good
home. However good the home is, it is bad for him or he
would be good! Parents and teachers often protest that they
treat the children "all alike!" thinking that this is impartial.
The only way to be truly impartial is to secure the right
reaction! We must constantly bear in mind that we are
dealing with a unit organism. As Henderson says, it is
impossible to have good health in one part of the organism
and ill health in another! It is either good or ill for the entire
organism always!

No one knows exactly the needs of childhood, or just how
to supply these, but even though the ideal may not be
realized at once it is still the high privilege and duty of the
adult to try to know. *The* way has not yet been found—the
last word has not been spoken. Skeptics sometimes ask,
"Will it fit my child?" There is no "it"—but an effort to
furnish the best conditions for every child. What those

needs are and how they are to be met may never be agreed upon, but we must continue to "reason together" and to study with an open mind. We do not present our program as final. The youngest teacher may find a better way. But we offer the following program as the best we have at this time. We group the children according to chronological age; this is really the only age of which we may be certain. We think this prevents self-consciousness and we believe the first condition of growth is unself-consciousness. Grouping children according to attainment or achievement gives a wrong conception of education. It gives the child the idea that education consists in meeting the demands of the adult. This self-consciousness may arrest development. Children should grow mentally as they do physically —without effort or strain. Grading makes the child think that an educated person is one who knows a great deal, or has unusual skill, or one who has met the requirements of the system and perhaps has received honors. Isn't it strange that we should feel it right and proper to reward people for learning? Some of the leaders in the progressive schools still contend that an external standard is necessary. Even in religion we constantly hear of a "crown" as the reward of faith or a good life, never realizing that the thought of the *reward* weakens the faith and disfigures the good life!

Learning is merely satisfying mental hunger. If society ever has rewards to offer they should be in recognition of a real contribution in actual service! And this is unnecessary, however, for whole-hearted, disinterested service is always its own reward! Therefore, it seems perfectly logical to eliminate the "reward" idea entirely. We shall never know how much real happiness and joy—yes, power—in the present has been lost, by this subtle fear of the future! This preparation idea!! Adults may fail to minister to growth but a child *cannot* fail. Even the idea of "measuring progress" may develop self-consciousness and be inhibiting—and furthermore, we all know that the *essential* in all progress is immeasurable!

The child should never feel that he must "keep up" with others mentally, any more than he should be stimulated to "keep up" in height or weight. When young children are grouped with older children they often feel superior to those of their own age and the child who is grouped with children much younger may acquire an inferiority complex. Still, it is always better for a child to be a little older than a little younger than his group. In the former case, he is more relaxed and gains poise and confidence. In the latter, he often suffers strain, which is especially undesirable for the growing child. The child who is fully the age of his group or a trifle older gets more out of his experience —is staying young—while the child grouped with older children is unable to benefit as fully from the experience and is *growing* old!

When the adolescent period is reached there is danger of forcing of the sex and social consciousness. As society becomes more complex, the period of childhood should be prolonged to preserve the power to adjust. The prolonging of childhood is the hope of the race—the longer the time from birth to maturity, the higher the organism. This is true individually as well as biologically. No parent should be proud of a precocious child. Intellectual "brilliance" in the very young may not be the promise of the finest maturity. Henderson says, "Children should be ignorant." This must be a great comfort to parents and teachers!

Children should not strive to get into a higher *grade*. Why should we subject the mental power of the child to measurements and external stimulation more than the physical or spiritual powers? If the body were subjected to the same conscious striving to meet external ends as those for which the mind is stimulated, all real physical vigor would be destroyed and such a process for the spirit would develop the most objectionable hypocrisy. When one sees children trying to "show off" their knowledge or skill, or insisting that certain children do not belong in their class, the elders are to be blamed, not the children. Sometimes children and even parents have complained because others who do not know as much or who have not done as fine work are promoted with them! We are hoping to forget the word "promoted." Education is the process of meeting the needs of children.

The teacher endeavors to provide activities and exercises which are adapted to the stage of development of the group, giving special attention to any individual child. This individual attention should never be of the kind that stimulates a child to "catch up" or "keep up" with the class—nor to "get ahead" or "keep ahead" of anyone—but merely to see that he clearly understands what he is doing. Not so much what one does, as the effect of the work on the pupil.

A college professor tells the story of a student coming to him one day and saying, "I know I am not doing very much this class and I know that you know I am not a good student; but I want you to know I am *getting more* out of this work than I ever did before."

All zest in learning depends upon mental grasp. If the work secures the best mental activity, it is educational. The observing eye of the teacher is necessary to discover when children are using their mental endowment to highest advantage. This is evidenced by eager and sustained interest and resulting satisfactions. It requires no test or examination to discover when children do their best at play. Neither should it be difficult to know when they are doing their best in school work.

The kindergarten is for children from four to six years of age. The session is only two hours. The room is large and

airy, furnished in the simplest way. There is no fixed
program, although the teacher keeps in mind that the
children need to have experience in musical expression,
daily singing and dancing, and musical games, and ample
time for free play. A playground is provided with a wading
pool, trees to climb, swings and slides, and plenty of space
for games. Children need time for quiet and rest—the story
hour. Stories should not be told for "language" nor for
"morals," but for the joy of the narrative. The story should
be full of action and adapted to the age of the children. No
special "method" is necessary; each teacher develops her
own method. All "method" is determined by two factors;
the aim and the nature of the material. The aim in
education is to provide conditions for children to live
wholesomely of body, using their minds to the best advantage and preserving the sincerity and unself-consciousness
of the emotional life. This requires a constant study of the
nature and needs of growth.

Much time is given to creative handwork, using clay,
sand, blocks, paints, and tools. The children have free
access to all material and the work is self-prompted and
self-directed. The presence of the material is suggestive.
Kindergarten children often live in an imaginary world
which is real to them. The fullest opportunity should be
given for this dramatization of life as long as it is in the right
direction.

When the child says "good-bye" to mother, his mind runs
forward to the activities of the school. If he finds the teacher
and other children engrossed in creative activity, he becomes interested at once to use material. The children in
our kindergarten and primary school are often so busily
employed before the opening hour that they do not know
whether school has "begun" or not! This gives them the
conception of school as a place to do things and the teacher
becomes a real friend who helps them to accomplish their
own purposes.

Time is given for dramatization and also for using some language other than their own, if the school can afford a teacher and if the children respond. Language should be used and incidentally learned. The speech centers are developed early, so that it is possible for a child to speak two or perhaps three languages wholesomely, whereas he should not learn to read or write on his own! If the teacher of French could remain in the school room for an hour, joining the children in their work and play, using French words occasionally, the children would become keen to "say something" in French also. Gradually and without any thought of a "French lesson" they would use the language in the presence of that teacher. In this way, a second language becomes a "means of communication," like the native tongue, and is never a task. I am always sorry for the children and for the French teacher when all work must stop to get ready for French! Too much time is spent in studying about a language, its form, construction, etc., when children are keen to use it.

There are aimless walks in which the teacher stops to discuss any object of interest. And also there are aimful walks for particular observation. Children *need* to have happy experiences with nature, not so much to learn facts as to acquire an attitude. "I saw a robin this morning," exclaims a child. "I found a white rose," cries another. "Oh, Miss F, let us go to see Mr. M's garden; ever so many things are growing and this is February." Children should not be held to close observation; no effort is made to teach, but it is very important that they play in the water and sand, have a garden or pets, throw stones, climb trees, and generally enjoy the out-of-doors. Even children of kindergarten age are interested in seeing what the rain did to the road—what animals and plants are doing and often why; while older children delight in tracing miniature river systems and learning about other forms of land and water. The great difficulty in all nature study is that teachers know so little

and care so little for the common things. Even those who
have majored in science in college are often at a loss when
walking with children. Unless they can have a text in their
hands, they often seem unable to recognize plants and
animals.

The knowledge gained in this way develops a confidence
in nature. Children should not be afraid of snakes, nor
toads, nor any creature—neither should they fear wind or
lightning or rain. "Let me put the snake around my neck!"
"Let me carry this big fellow in my blouse!" Of course, the
teacher must allow the children to handle only harmless
snakes!

At six years of age, we put them in what we call the
"first-life" class. A "life class" is where children live as
wholesomely, happily, and intelligently as possible, and
incidentally learn something. We do not want to be under
any obligation to the parents for what they learn. Two very
amazing attitudes persist among adults; first, that education is identical with erudition and skill; second, that the
more rapidly a child can be piloted through the grades, the
better for all concerned.

We believe that through happy, wholesome, intelligent
experiences learning takes place. One of the most persist-
ent questions of parents is: "Will my child be *ready* for the
next grade when he goes back home?" Usually the children
return to their grade in the conventional school with no
apparent loss and very often with a noticeable increase of
power. Children who have been in this school for some
years and are obliged to leave are sometimes graded quite
beyond their years in other schools. One father complained
that his child did nothing but "play" in our school because
she had no homework, but later, when she entered another
school, he reported that she had surpassed the other
children of her class and had been allowed to "skip" a grade.
Of course, the explanation is that the "play" of which he

complained gave her opportunity for inner growth, coordination, and integration which manifested as power a little later. They are often noticeable for their frank interest in things, their initiative and poise. Said one mother, "The teacher asked what school my child had attended, saying that he was eager and showed a finer mental grasp than others and was more dependable."

The musical program for the six and seven-year-olds consists of songs, singing games, and folk dancing, with varied rhythmic and dramatic expression often inspired by the story. We believe that singing is merely another form of saying something. Children should sing and dance and be filled with musical feeling before an attempt is made to use an instrument or read notes! The usual process in teaching music is to place notes before the child, helping him to read by identifying the note with the keyboard. After considerable experience he learns to *hear*. The process should be singing, hearing, first, being filled with musical sounds, then gradually using the keyboard by ear, then at last identifying the sound with the sight of the notes! Happily many music teachers are following the newer process of filling the child with musical feeling through the use of his voice, then the instrument, and finally the notes. We try to postpone the teaching of musical symbols until at least ten years of age. Children should hear and feel music long before the eye is trained to read notes.

The session is now three hours and the work is considerably strengthened. The stories may be those of myths, fables, folklore, and fairy tales; also, stories of information, such as animal stories and other stories of nature. The teacher uses her own method. All method is determined by the aim, knowledge of the material, and of childhood. The aim is to keep the children occupied intelligently, and the knowledge of childhood and the material increases with study and experience.

Children should not be over-stimulated, neither should they be bored. Sometimes parents complain that their children suffer from lack of intellectual stimulus. On investigation, it is invariably found that the children have not developed initiative and feel that they are not "learning" because tasks are not assigned. We think the assignment of tasks often results in immoral experiences— therefore, this is postponed until high school. Things that *move* one in the wrong direction are immoral. Homework usually moves both mother and child in the wrong direction! The mother gets nervous and is irritated when demands from the school interfere with her home plans, and the child often uses the school tasks as an excuse for neglecting the mother's requests. But the temptation to *appear* to know when he doesn't know, is perhaps the most weakening and thus immoral part of the child's experience. While children are not conscious of set tasks, they understand perfectly that they are expected to do whatever the teacher wishes them to do. The teacher, however, may learn the art of allowing children full opportunity for self-prompted work without the danger of trifling and disorder.

Stories are told, and the children may tell stories to the group. Stories are not used, however, for "language lessons," but frankly for the joy of the story. Marionette shows are popular in this group. They enjoy making the little theater, out of a box usually, arranging curtains, making scenery and the puppets. Then, most exciting of all—giving the show! A deer hunt, when the teacher remains at home to receive the game and enjoy the feast, is a great experience for six and seven-year-olds. "You better not go with us," explains a child to the teacher, "because we are going through barb wire fences, briars, and down in holes"; then, reassuringly, "but you can take the deer when we drive it in."

Most of the dramatic work of this group is quite spontaneous. A group sometimes asks the teacher to take the rest of the children out of the room while they get ready to give a play! "Don't tell them what we are going to do, but please take them out until we call you." So often teachers fear to grant requests lest "all the others may want to do the same thing." This rarely occurs, and if it should, the teacher should be able to meet it. Children must know that their requests *will* be granted whenever it is wise or possible. This deep, well-founded confidence in the adult is a vital factor in the development of personality in the child. A sense of security prevents self-consciousness.

Fundamental conceptions of numbers are given the seven-year-old group if the teacher is able to secure a satisfactory response—otherwise, numbers may be postponed until eight years of age. These consist of weighing, measuring, counting, using the ruler, but no use of figures. The use of figures is often a barrier to the mind in gaining number conceptions.

Children think that three-fourths is merely a three with four under it. When the right *conception* of number is acquired, we find children *using* numbers constantly in their leisure and in play. "I'm going to take this home and see if Daddy can make a picture of a third of a fourth." One little boy, after "dividing things up," exclaimed, "A fourth of a fourth of a fourth is an awfully small thing, isn't it?"

There is no reading or writing in this group, since this may interfere with nerve growth and it is a severe form of specialized activity unsuited for children at this age. When the entire organism is in a state of exceedingly rapid activity and change, arrest of development may easily take place. We believe the omission of the use of books for little children results in better thinking. If the schools were frankly engaged in trying to meet the needs of the growing child, no doubt they would insist upon every child having experience in singing, dancing, handwork, stories, and nature. This work adapted to the age of children would fill the day full of happy, wholesome occupation.

The child who reads early learns to rely upon the printed page for authority and may fail lamentably to understand the meaning of his experiences! The entire race seems quite unable to learn from experience! Isn't it strange that so many people feel there is little or no *learning* except from books? In fact, they often speak of the "tools of learning," meaning symbols. When one considers the immense amount of learning that takes place before the child reaches school age, it is surprising that such emphasis is placed upon books as *tools* of *learning!*

Reading should be postponed until ten years of age. If children were allowed to think through experience, a tendency to wait for data, to search for truth and use it for authority, might be developed. Children tend to act on thinking. This is intelligence. Excessive or too early use of books may interfere. The use of books too early often develops an unsocial attitude. Children are entertained by reading stories when they should be working creatively or playing with others. Many children become quite unfit to live with others as a result of sitting for hours in a bad light, bad position, passively being entertained by a book! The bragging, bossy, irritable, unhappy, self-centered child is quite apt to be the child who reads excessively. We have had children whose behavior was positively subnormal caused by too constant use of books—utterly lacking in ability to meet situations. "My child cannot do anything with his hands, and he enjoys being with adults much more than playing with children," says a perplexed mother.

While information is not the aim in nature study, at this age children are interested to know many things that might escape the notice of younger children. Snakes and toads and all animals are attractive to children if the observation is not pressed upon them. The living creature is studied through actual contact, rather than lessons about them. Gardens are very interesting and excursions and walks and all-day picnics are popular. Our bay is a never-exhausted attraction. Here they may dig in the sand to their hearts' content, wade and sail their little boats, build dams, make lakes, waterfalls, islands, and all forms of land and water. The gullies are always stimulating to dramatic or investigating impulses. "Let's play the gods! I'm Jupiter—I'm Juno—I'm Minerva!" shout the children as they troop to the gully. Many happy hours have been spent in the gully dramatizing the old Greek myths and other stories, while the teacher lazily sits on a log in the sun.

Handwork holds a very prominent place on the program, being almost wholly self-prompted and self-directed. Work in color is very fascinating for these children. They love to illustrate poems or stories, using large sheets of paper, large brushes and vivid water colors. Much work in clay is also done quite independently, though the teacher's help is sometimes solicited. But the great joy of children of this age is wood-working. They never tire of the jig-saw, plane, hammer and nails, and sometimes the lathe, and many happy and profitable hours are spent using tools and soft wood. What do they make and how well is the work done? They make many objects for use and some things are well done, but the work is successful if the children enjoy the activity and experience real satisfaction. "Just think, Mother," exclaims a new boy, "You can make what you want, and you can take it home!" They sometimes need help to persist until an object is finished, and occasionally articles begun may be abandoned. Occasionally parents think that since reading is not taught at this age, excellent handwork should be produced! "I don't send my child to school to pound nails," said a disgusted mother, removing her child. "He can do that at home."

Children have not the nervous coordination nor control
necessary for finished work. All children's work is characterized by the imperfections due to their undeveloped state.
"This," said the teacher, handing a photograph to a visitor,
"is work done by six-year-olds without suggestion or
direction." The visitor, glancing at the picture, handed it
back saying, "It looks it!" Again we repeat, all work must be
judged by the spirit of the worker.

In this machine age, the greatest responsibility rests on
the schools for developing the power and inclination to use
leisure profitably! If inner satisfaction and consciousness of
power are experienced through the growing years in
creative work, the profitable use of leisure is assured. A
young man built his own house, saying proudly, "I learned
that in old Organic!" All children below the high school are
given two periods daily in shop and craft work. The creative
mind is one that is critical in the best sense—that is, seeking
the truth and taking it for authority. It is also the mind that
is tolerant, charitable to his neighbor. When one is engaged
in absorbingly interesting work, he hasn't time to keep a
negatively critical eye on his neighbor, and if he should
perchance recognize mistakes in his neighbor, he knows
that he too has often failed to reach his ideal. So with a
humble spirit he sympathizes instead of condemning.

The standard is an inner, human one. If the work is
suitable and wholesome and the children delight in it, there
is growth, which is the essence of education. Dewey says
education is "vital energy seeking opportunity for effective
exercise." Surely we must agree that it is wholesome,
interested activity with consequent satisfactions. Finish and
technique come later. The teacher has a program, but she is
not obliged to follow it. The whole morning may be spent in
the gully, at the bay, or in the woods without a guilty
conscience! Much time is given to free play. In many schools
direction, even in play, is so constant that children rarely
experience the absence of external demands long enough

to allow the "inner necessity" to develop! Henderson bemoans the fact that people seem driven by fear, poverty, ignorance, but most of all they are driven by the absence of a redeeming idea! The child always has a redeeming idea until his elders direct, instruct, and thwart his efforts until the inner impulse is destroyed. Behavior and other "problem children" have made remarkable progress in overcoming limitations merely through the "removal of external pressure."

At eight years of age they enter the "second-life" class. Learning to read, write and spell is now added to the program of arts and crafts, wood-working, singing, folk dancing, and nature. Here stories of history, literature, and geography are given. The stories of children of other lands and the making of maps are absorbing. Children should have experiences making maps or plans of rooms, buildings, etc., on the ground, then on paper, emphasizing the points of the compass—then lastly, picking the map up by the north end and hanging it on the wall that they may realize that a stream may flow *down* north! And that the "top" of the map is not always "up" on the ground. I have seen sixth grade children trace "down" a river from the sea inland!

Instead of a reading lesson, there is a "library period" in which all the children who know how to read enjoy reading books of their own choosing, the teacher assisting those who need help. Very few children need much help in learning to read if it is postponed until eight or nine years of age, for many of them have already "picked it up." In some cases where learning to read is postponed, the children have needed no instruction at all! But when help is needed the teacher should use the very best method, that the art may be acquired as quickly and as easily as possible.

They now begin the use of figures in their number work, learning the simpler mechanics and to read and write numbers. At this age children delight in the manipulation of figures, and in rapid work in combinations. Care is used to prevent the nervousness and self-consciousness that often develop in this work. Many slowly developing little people have suffered intensely in time tests! "I know how to do it, Mother, but I get so excited when the teacher holds her watch!" No doubt many an inferiority complex has been acquired by a child who is unable to get the answer in time! And no doubt many children have developed a tendency to "jump at answers" or misrepresent! No "tests" should ever be given! The thought of failure should be unknown! Children may be encouraged to work rapidly and accurately without the nerve-racking experience of "time tests."

Reasoning problems and those requiring analysis are postponed until at least twelve years of age, and even here we often find children still unable to follow through problems requiring the conscious reasoning involved in profit and loss.

The conversation in some other language than their own is continued if a teacher able to lead can be secured. Very few teachers have the understanding and ability to prevent the use of another language from becoming a "lesson." They have been trained in the use of devices to produce "results." It will bear repeating that language is a tool—a *means,* not an end. It should never be *studied, learned,* and *recited,* but should rather be *used* and incidentally acquired! Children of this age delight in talking and learning how to say things in French, if it is done informally and in connection with the common things in which they are interested and if their attention is not demanded for too long at one time.

Nature study not only is continued in this group for the development of an attitude, but now is a source of real information. The group may make a collection of leaves, seeds, stones, or even snakes! If this is wisely done, all fear of snakes is utterly destroyed. To carry a large, twisting, squirming snake around one's neck, with its tongue lapping one's face, is an experience developing courage and self-control. One also acquires a marvelous feeling toward such creatures which no amount of exhortation to kindness could ever secure. The *feeling* of ownership and affection needs no exhortation to develop the attitude of kindness and protection.

The facts of physical geography are studied first-hand in the gullies, at the bay shore, in the woods, and acquaintance is made with the animals of the neighborhood, their activities and importance. Much attention is paid to the adaptation of the plants and animals to their environment. The study of nature's methods of seed distribution is most stimulating and delightful.

All sorts of questions must be answered: Why did the water drop the sand here, and pebbles there? Let us pile up a barrier here to see if the water will drop its sand the next time it rains. The gullies already formed and in the forming furnish the finest stimulation to investigation, thought, and observation. How do you know the water was running swiftly here? Where are the tributaries to these rivers? Let us find a water-shed or an island. Why are there drops of water on the wire when there are no drops on my hand? What makes the wind blow? Why does the smoke go up the chimney? Where does the tadpole's tail go and which legs come first? Of what use is a snake? Why should we protect the turtles? How do the birds help us? Why does the tree grow pears? What may we find growing in the garden in December in this climate? Let us keep a record of things growing in the South each month. How do they compare with those in the North? These and countless other questions occupy the attention of the children during the nature period. A child from another school said, "I hate nature" but was soon fascinated by the intimate, informal

approach and exclaimed, "Oh, but I love to do this!" Some
children are sure they do not have nature study in the
school because it is not labeled and conducted as a lesson. It
is a great pity that "courses of study" have developed the
wrong attitude toward and the wrong conception of education. The aim is to awaken the spirit of inquiry and the
desire to understand. Gardens constitute a most interesting
part of the naure study. They plant vegetables and
flowers—each child having a plot of his own.

Stories must continue to be told to this group since the
children are still in the process of learning to read. Often
stories in geography, history, or literature are worked out
in the shop or craft room in the form of projects. The
teacher of the group cooperates with the teacher in the
shop, so that the work in the manual training often becomes
a continuation of the interest already developed in the
school room.

The "project," however, is not obliged to furnish the
means of acquiring subject matter or skill, though these
often do result. Projects may be undertaken for the pure joy
of the experience. Parents are so wedded to the idea that
educaion is identical with learning facts that teachers often
feel obliged to point out that reading, writing, spelling,
geography, or some other "subject matter" is being acquired in the project. One year, the children illustrated the
Amazon region. They made the animals, the vines, the
forests, and had a wonderful time placing bread pans end
to end for the river, and many people in town came to see it.

A Japanese project consumed many happy days. At last a
"fete" was given at which everyone dressed as Japanese.
Fans, screens, kites, and even jinrikishas to carry people to
the little shrines on the hillside, were made in the shop. No
doubt the Japanese would smile at such imitations—but this
study was good because the children not only enjoyed the
activity and received some information, but best of all, they

acquired a friendly attitude, a kindly, sympathetic feeling—that is, they were moved in the right direction, which constitutes a moral experience.

Much time is given to singing the old folk songs, and the children now delight in learning the folk dances. A great musician once said that the very best possible preparation for the appreciation of the great masters of music is to be *steeped* in folk song! The spirit of the folk and that of the *great* master are identical!

We believe the folk dance is better adapted to the school room than any other form of dancing. The folk dance is the fundamental, elemental unself-conscious expression of the folk and belongs especially to the young and the old whose spirit is still young. It is simple—few, if any, steps to learn. It is objective and purposeful, it is highly social and very beautiful. It does not require a special costume, only a little space. Afternoon parties are often given, the program consisting of games and folk dancing, with parents invited and light refreshments served. We believe all evening functions for children younger than high school age should be discouraged. Social relations as well as school activities should be kept simple and unsophisticated.

The children of eight and nine years of age have had two years of growth through the use of music, dancing, dramatics, wood-working, arts and crafts, nature, free play, and stories, and have learned as much of reading, writing, spelling, and numbers as they could learn wholesomely and happily.

The work in music in this group deserves special mention. It consists in singing the old English folk and other songs. The joy of the children in singing these songs that "tell a story," the beauty of the tone and the spirit of the singers receive the most favorable attention. Singing is really a form of talking—and everyone should sing!

The school day has been four hours long, given to varied

interesting occupations, with two hours at noon for lunch and rest and play. We have always insisted that at least one half-hour be spent in perfect quiet after the noon meal. There is no fixed curriculum, but the teacher keeps a simple record of work done as a guide to the next teacher. The teacher must also feel free from external pressure. Personality, poise, resourcefulness, and power—the qualities most essential to the good teacher—are often thwarted, stultified, throttled, prevented from developing, by the harrowing, nerve-racking external pressure of the demands of the "system."

Bell Building—Tolling of Bell Announces
Beginning of School Day and Class Changes

Working with Clay

Solving a Chemistry Problem

Old English Sword Dance

The Kentucky Running Set

Building a Log Cabin

Climbing Tree

Looking for a Camp Site

What a Beautiful Location!

1945 City Champs and Cheer Leaders

Spring Festival Pole Dance

An Outdoor Classroom

A Partial View of the Campus

A Christmas Play

The Start of a New Day

Classroom Scene

5   OLDER CHILDREN

The ten- and eleven-year-old group is called the "third life" class. The children have been learning to read, write, spell, and use figures. Now they almost, if not quite fully, are able to use "tools" independently. Most of them may now read their own stories, though they still enjoy and profit by hearing stories told by the teacher. They are still growing in the great art of listening. The child should never enter the ten-year-old group until he is fully ten, even though he may *know* enough to "do the work" of the eleven-year-olds. Time for relaxation, poise, coordination, and integration are demands of childhood which the school is obligated to meet.

In the early years of the school the rule was that all children of ten, or going to be ten before Christmas, comprised the group—but experience taught us that it is better for even a precocious child to be fully the age of the group, or older. Thus, every child would be fully fourteen or nearly fifteen before entering the high school. It was not easy for all to adjust to this idea for it destroyed the "expectations" of some parents and for a time there was complaining all along the line—and a few who claimed full accord with the principle, doubted the wisdom of its educational system; for fear of being "kept back" and eagerness to "get ahead" persists in adults and is transmitted to children in spite of full acceptance of the new point of view.

Creative handwork in this group continues in both shop and craft room. The projects are often stimulated by the social studies. But the project is conducted for itself rather than to "acquire" certain subject matter, though factual knowledge often results. Too often, even in progressive schools, teachers are conscious of the necessity of "getting over" certain facts, of "showing results" in knowledge and skill, of reaching some external standard! This is the standard of attainment and achievement which is believed to be "measureable." As an educational philosopher remarked, "We have many new methods, new devices, but our standard remains the same." Of course, much knowledge is gained and this is the time to acquire skill in the use of books and figures, as well as in creative handwork. But keenness of interest, concentration, and perseverance for immediate ends in cooperation with one's fellows is the finest "subject matter" at this age.

An Andes railroad was once constructed in the gullies. A very good miniature of the Panama Canal was also built. The Siege of Troy and other Greek myths were dramatized in the gully, which furnishes natural eminences for the gods and goddesses. The children spent weeks studying and dramatizing the life of gypsies, while another group played Indian. The gypsies "stole a child" and the Indians dashed to the rescue. Indian tepees were made, and a gypsy camp maintained.

The children are now old enough to engage in cooking and sewing. This work is not undertaken to acquire technique in either art, but rather to use them as means to ends. To make muffins for a party, candy for refreshments, making aprons for working in clay, decorating curtains for the room, are projects of immediate fascinating interest. We try to keep in mind all the time that the true ends of education are always human and immediate, never remote or material. All learning and skills must minister to growth—human power—and may never be acquired at the expense of power. True intelligence, adapting means to ends, meeting situations, are never more truly developed than through such experiences. "In June we see many young people emerging from our institutions with diplomas in their hands and weakness in their bodies." In all forms of handwork the children are now ready to give more attention to technique.

History, literature, and geography are read and enjoyed, the group sitting about a table and discussing, the teacher making the work as vital as possible through pictures, illustrations, or other embellishments. It is far more important that children shall love history, literature, and geography, than any particular amount of subject matter shall be mastered.

In this group attention is given to writing poetry and short stories; letters are written, records kept, and sometimes a paper is published. This affords the teacher full opportunity to emphasize expression and spelling. Sometimes an old-fashioned "spelling match" is enjoyed and often lists of words are studied and written. These words are usually those that have been misspelled, or words they are using immediately. Sometimes a "spelling book" is made by the children, the words being arranged alphabetically, and they enjoy comparing their books with one another, seeing how many words begin with "A" or "G". The mechanics of number continues, the aim being to enjoy the use of figures in attaining accuracy and rapidity. Fundamental conceptions of number are not neglected, however. Children of this age are often able to show how many two-thirds there are in three-fourths without the use of figures. They are as keen to divide by "four figures" in the divisor, to add rapidly, to learn tables and become as efficient in the use of figures as the most conservative teacher might desire, even when no external pressure is applied! Fractions and decimals are enjoyed—and, of course, the multiplication table becomes a ready tool.

Dramatics are an important part of the progress. More attention is paid to the lines, although many original productions are given. The children of this age are also more critical and require better stage setting, properties, etc. Every class is a free discussion of the matter in hand. There are no desks in any of the rooms and no assignment of tasks. No examinations are given, nor tests, nor homework. There are no report cards. We believe that three or four hours daily in directed work is enough for children of this age. A considerable part of this time should be given to self-prompted creative work. Home tasks are objectionable from every point of view. Carrying books hampers the child's free movement in going to and from school. The thought of a requirement of the school often interferes with his entering freely into the home situation and may cause friction. The conscientious child is burdened with a feeling of guilt in case of failure to prepare the homework. He learns that it is for his interest to *appear* to know.

The session for the ten- and eleven-year-old children is two hours and a half in the morning and an hour and a half in the afternoon. We like to have children approach their school work with the same enthusiasm that is evident in play. We believe children of this age should have long hours in the open, free from demands of the school, and also time to dream.

Education should not be identified with meeting requirements and keeping up—but, rather, school should be a place for good times—a place to do many things—and the teacher is a person who helps. Sometimes children new in the school think they are not "learning" much because no lessons are assigned and no marks given. But soon they forget all about marks and tasks and enter into the immediate situation with abandon and consequent joy. Education then may finally become identified with wholesome, happy, intelligent activity!

They continue to use some other language than their own, adhering strictly to the conversational method. There should be absolutely nothing given in this group that could possibly be called grammar—nor even language lessons! Much time is given to music and dancing. Great pleasure is found in singing the old English folk songs and dancing the folk dances. The folk song always tells a story. It is rhythmical, dramatic, jolly, fascinating, and beautiful. It belongs to childhood. Many parents have expressed their delight in hearing their children singing alone and in groups at home and elsewhere in play. This group is able to dance the most intricate English country folk dances and to enjoy the Morris dances. Sometimes the children compose new dances. Every effort is made to furnish the fullest opportunity for ample social life without evening affairs, which are unwholesome for children below high school age.

All pupils must use their mental power to highest advantage. We feel that it is more important that they should think through things and preserve the freshness of intellectual attack than it is, perhaps, to amass a great fund of information or to acquire unusual skill, though these are not neglected. Even in book work, if the child is not conscious of the expectation of the teacher, he often gives expression to most interesting and original thought. "Yes," said a boy from the country, in discussing cooperation, "unless the horses pull together, you never get anywhere!" At this age, children are fond of keeping scores in games and physical feats, though no prizes are given—no public attention is called to the winner!

The spirit of competition is always dangerous. A little boy won a running match. "What did you get?" asked his neighbor. "Why, I WON," replied the boy. It never occurred to him that anything could be added to the fun of winning. After thinking it over, later he volunteered, "I think if any prize is ever given, it should be given to the one who didn't win!" It must be assumed that children are sincere in all their work and play, and only sympathy and encouragement should be given those who do not win in sports, and also to those who perhaps do not acquire the arts of reading, writing, and the use of figures as readily as others.

We teach no particular form of penmanship, but pay attention to legibility. We do not subject the children to tests or measurements. The consciousness of an immediate external necessity is not conducive to poise or clear thinking and may become a real repression. It is unfortunate that adults are obliged to work under such pressure, but the undeveloped child should be protected from all nerve-racking experiences. "I never dominate the children, I never hurry them," said a self-satisfied teacher. "See how happy they are." Then as an after thought, she cried, "Children, as you go out show the visitor how many of you passed!" The line then formed and those who had "passed" walked with arms folded on chests and heads up, while the others walked with hands behind their backs and drooping heads! Intellectual development should be as free from self-consciousness and strain as physical growth. The real test of the work is in the *attitude* of the children. If they are interested and sincere in their work and study and the activity is wholesome, they are having an educational experience. The child is never conscious of having to do any particular thing in order to pass into the next class. "I am ten, I'm going in Third Life," exclaims the ten-year-old. He knows that when he is twelve years old, he will go into the twelve-year-old group. This has never had an undesirable effect upon interest or effort. Since desire to "pass" has never been an incentive to study, it is not necessary to resort to it as a stimulation. In fact, the idea of passing or not passing seems never to enter their minds. Children should not be burdened with thoughts of failure or success. It is a joy to be alive and active. There is keen delight in intellectual activity and the children should experience this. They are enjoying the work or study, they are using their minds—that is enough.

Eventually parents recognize the signs of unselfconscious growth and are thankful for such signs in their children. One of our children, hearing his little friend from another school exclaiming: "I got an A" asked, "What is that?" "Why," replied his friend, "that means I stood high, I have a fine mark, I did good work." "Oh," said the child, "I never heard of such a thing!" and the mother rejoiced.

The argument has often been made that children will not work or study unless obliged to do so. Many teachers testify to this, but always upon investigation it is found that these children who "will not study unless compelled to do so" usually are very keen, even self-sacrificingly so, in matters where interest has been aroused. To arouse interest, to keep the mind stimulated, is the art of the teacher. The teacher found a group of children remaining after school. "What is it you are doing?" she queried. "Why," replied the children, "we are going to give a play tomorrow and are getting ready." "I can't be late," protested a boy to his mother, "because I'll lose my history." The teacher was using the time-honored method of teaching history through stories!

Teachers often take themselves too seriously, they take the work too seriously, they are too conscious of standards of work and behavior. "They've just got to do a month's work in a month," exclaimed an irritable teacher who found it difficult to hold attention without pressure. It is true that an indifferent teacher is always deplorable, but a teacher may be jolly and free and human—and should really *enjoy* his work. "I like Miss K outside school," cried a child. "She is fun at a party—but oh, how strict and sober she is in school!!"

Of course, many children are weak in power of concentration, and assistance may be needed at times to prevent trifling and fooling; but given work suited to their development and an earnest teacher understanding children, as well as the subject, we find that they do concentrate and acquire information and skill without recourse to external goals of accomplishment—passing—or threats of failure!

The situation is sufficient to secure good work and the satisfaction in the activity is sufficient reward! A little girl from another school constantly called attention to herself and her work, and sometimes was guilty of glaring falsehoods, so anxious was she to secure the favorable attention of the adults! Such a spirit could never have developed without the external standard in the minds of both teacher and pupil!

We believe even more is accomplished in the so-called subject matter when enjoying it from day to day without any thought of requirements, than could possibly be done under pressure—and we believe that the absence of pressure is absolutely essential to growth. We do not encourage children to measure themselves. This is apt to develop self-consciousness which must dull the edge of real learning. "I often talk over the work with the children helping them to compare today's results with former work," said an earnest though mistaken teacher. When one is thinking of his rate of intellectual progress or increase in skill, his mind is divided. He should be able to concentrate utterly upon the activity. Learning is satisfying mental hunger as eating is satisfying physical hunger. If we were obliged to keep track of their learning, nausea and indigestion would certainly result. I wonder if children's withdrawal from the learning program of the schools may not be due to this mental indigestion which may follow the conscious effort of learning.

If they have enjoyed facts and have thought through cause and effect with concentration and with resulting satisfaction—they are growing, being educated, and to measure that experience would be to weaken it.

At twelve or thirteen years of age the children automatically pass into the fourth-life class. Here the session is a little longer, being three and one-half hours in the morning and an hour and a half in the afternoon. The work for this group is about the same as that given to any seventh or eighth grade in other schools. The children like to be called "Junior High," though there is no special reason for this. Nature study is now called Elementary Science and this work is often conducted by the high school teacher of science. In fact, the tendency is to departmentalize the work of this group, thought we make an effort to keep these children as simple and unsophisticated as possible.

Literature, history, and geography are studied as literature, although larger projects are now undertaken in history and geography and much work is done in the study of invention, discovery, and industry. Greek plays are given out of doors and excellent reproductions of Greek art done in clay are sometimes presented by this group. There is no "course of study" to be followed in any particular order in successive years. The teacher is free to emphasize any particular period or phase, always being careful not to repeat the work of the previous year. These children may work in leather and metals as well as wood, clay, and color. Very often artistic talent is discovered. Much time is devoted to writing and talking. The children often decide whether they wish to write or talk. Then, while one division engages in written work, the teacher takes the other group off for free discussion. Some attention is given to form and this may be their introduction to grammar. We believe that grammar, however, belongs in the high school and college. So often children are dumb in a language lesson, but exceedingly talkative among their friends out of school. The consciousness of *form* is always inhibiting. Perhaps the analysis of sentence construction belongs at the college level! Children should have ample opportunity and encouragement for the fullest, freest expression of their thought, without fear of criticism. The art of expression is encouraged throughout the elementary school, but the analysis of construction comes later.

In arithmetic a book is now used with applied problems for the first time and all are eager to engage in such work. This requires analysis, for which these children are usually quite ready and eager. Not a great deal of such work is given and no pressure used where children are not quite ready. The analysis of a problem, which is really a situation involving the principle of cause and effect, is quite different from the analysis of sentence construction. The use of fundamental conceptions of number is continued, in fact we find it profitable to refer to "fundamentals" constantly, even in the high school. The main work, however, is that of getting facility in finding and solving all sorts of problems. Much work in the mechanics of number is also given. Sometimes children in this group become interested to use algebraic formulas in solving problems. One eminent educator suggests that arithmetic be omitted entirely as a subject of study in the elementary school. The intelligent use of number in all projects, manual training, and other crafts should be encouraged, but formal mathematics might begin in the high school with the study of algebra! We do not follow this suggestion, but it helps us to realize that arithmetic need not be "completed" or "mastered" before high school is reached.

No child is required to do any particular amount of work in order to continue in his group. The teacher's effort is to keep every child keenly interested and doing the best work possible for him. In cases of superior ability, more work is provided or extra time allowed in crafts, but they are not grouped with older children.

Our shop is the largest, most attractive building on the grounds. Here are three large rooms: one for work in clay—one for weaving, metal working, color, and leather—and a still larger one for wood-working. All are very light, airy, and comfortable and every child in the elementary school spends two periods daily in the shop. It is always a disappointment to me to find the shops in the basement in so many schools, with inadequate space and inadequate light. There is not as yet the whole-hearted recognition of the arts in education. Often children may be allowed to omit this work altogether. The emphasis is still too much on academic results!

Larger objects, such as tables and chairs, are undertaken, the work being in response to some real need. While some attention is now given to finish and technique, great care is used to prevent discouragement by criticism. It is very important that critical power does not exceed executive ability. Boats and kites are very popular and "kite day" is almost as exciting an occasion as some regular holiday. To see the sky clouded by kites of all sizes and shapes, and some of great beauty, to see the faces of the children and grown-ups as they guide their kites through the air, makes one feel that we have really arrived! But when one thinks of what "people will say," one is frightened to death! A boat launching also affords the keenest pleasure. Even though the adults who are invited to ride do get wet feet and may be in danger of capsizing—still no one could refuse to venture in these hand-made boats. Of course, models of airplanes are very popular and many hours at home as well as at school are happily occupied in this work. Many boys are interested in automobile construction. Old parts gathered in the village, with the teacher's help, are evolved into a rather respectable car named "the Rolls-Rejoice!!"

Folk dancing and singing are continued, the children being now old enough to learn to read notes and sing simple part songs. These children join the glee club and every child that can possibly play an instrument enters the orchestra. One of the great rewards to the school is that of seeing children persuading their parents to allow them to take private lessons in music on the piano or violin in order to do better work in the school orchestra, and then noting the later blossoming of these young musicians!

Carol singing at Christmas and invitations to present choruses and demonstrate folk dances at social functions are enjoyed. We do not approve of exhibitions, but a demonstration which emphasizes the dance—not the dancers—and may stimulate others to desire to participate, is quite permissible. A special fete day in March has long been observed. Here a full program of country and Morris dancing is given, and these children do as well and enjoy it as much as the older pupils in the high school.

We sometimes say that we do not teach music or dancing, arts, nor academic subjects, neither do we teach children;

but rather, provide conditions for children to express themselves—to grow *through* these activities! The time must soon arrive when the emphasis in all schools will be placed upon the effect of the activity upon the student rather than upon external results!

The work in literature is used as a basis for dramatics, although impromptu plays are sometimes given, marionette shows, and very often plays of their own composition are presented. The little outdoor theater is in constant use and sometimes these children present a play of their own composition in the hall. Usually, however, all dramatics at this age are simple, and given in the daytime with no admission charges!

No child may fail, no work is ever "made up." The children may go on hikes or camping trips, and even whole days are consumed in this way. An effort is made to allow no child to enter the high school until he is fully fourteen, nearly or quite fifteen being preferred.

History continues to be history stories, with the emphasis perhaps on American History. This group, during the two years, usually reads books of Greek and Roman History, some stories of medieval times, and enjoys American history stories, as well as those of invention and industry.

There are no tests or examinations—no requirements for promotion. It is a mistake to insist upon certain scholastic requirements for entrance into the high school. If a child of fourteen or fifteen has the social development and mental grasp of that age, he can do the work in the high school even if he has "failed" in every subject of the eighth grade! In case he has not done the requisite work in arithmetic, he may be quite able to begin algebra. If he has not had the eighth grade history, he can readily study ancient history, and if he knows little of geography he can still study physical geography or general science. In the case of English, he is perfectly able to study literature with his group, and he can begin the study of grammar, if desired.

The adolescent period is here and an effort is made to have the relation of the sexes simple, direct, and unself-conscious. Afternoon and early evening parties are often devised. Groups of mothers arrange these parties. Sometimes they are given on the school grounds, sometimes in the homes, but games are played and there is folk dancing, and refreshments are served. The children have had two or three hours of free, happy, unsophisticated association with one another and are at home and ready for bed before nine o'clock.

Children should gradually develop a consciousness of their responsibility to one another. We cannot teach or train a social consciousness—it is a matter of growth through social experiences. When children work, play, study together, reacting to one another, not merely to the teacher, there develops the most desirable interdependent spirit. Dewey says that when an individual thinks he can stand alone, he is suffering from an unnamed form of insanity. A social atmosphere is preserved in all of the work of the school.

We believe that sex instruction should be given at the proper time; that is, when the child asks questions. This usually occurs in the home at an early age and the mother is the natural source of information, though the father should share this responsibility. If the parents have not already given this instruction, then the teacher should do so and it should be done preferably in the lower grades. Nature study is the natural medium. But if the teacher of the twelve- and thirteen-year olds is obliged to instruct the children, it should be done in a most matter-of-fact, scientific way, and care should be taken to avoid all sentimentality or unhealthy association.

Teachers coming from other schools have often remarked about the absence of fighting among the children and the absence of vulgar talk and obscenity. Perhaps direct instruction should be given individually to avoid the unwholesome suggestion which may be made by any member of the group. This requires wisdom and discretion on the part of the teacher, but it may not be neglected or postponed!

These children have an hour and a half at noon. We believe it is very important at this stage in their development that time should be given to masticate and insalivate their food, and some time for rest after the noon meal. It is not always easy to get parents to cooperate in this matter of a noonday rest. Too often the children dash through luncheon and are back on the school grounds before one o'clock! The hurried lunch hour of many schools is very detrimental to health. In many consolidated schools, the lunch period is very short. This is necessary on account of the long bus ride after school. Would it not be wiser to shorten the time of study and give time for the recreation necessary for health? But the demands of the system, the "units" necessary for college entrance forbid! At this time when the reproductive organs are developing functional power, ample time should be given for digestion and assimilation.

The afternoon session closes at three o'clock, with no lessons assigned for the next day. All conceptions come through experience. If the school constantly makes external demands, the children come to believe that education is attained when demands are met. They should realize that education is growth—a gradual unfolding through happy, interested, wholesome activity.

The pupils may go home free to engage in any activity —or, they may remain on the school grounds for sports or free play. We believe the home is sometimes educational and often interesting. If education is life, then life is also education and learning is something that happens to one in the course of experiences. Why should not learning take place at home as well as at school? In an agricultural school, the teacher would not give "credit" for raising a fine crop of corn at home, though raising corn was in the curriculum! It must be done *under* the *direction* of the school to be of educational value! Isn't it strange that we have built up an educational system, which is often unwise, unjust, and sometimes injurious, defeating our avowed aim—and still we are unable to change it, or even to modify it to meet most urgent needs?

The creative work often overflows into the home life. Many children take material home from the school to work on during leisure time. We are always delighted when this occurs, and consider it a most happy and desirable result of the school's activities. "My child is making Christmas Cards at home," or "My children work all the time at home making things," is often heard. Sometimes projects begun at home are brought to school to be finished. The mending of couches, or caning of chairs, making of nets for fishing—and at one time the mending of shoes could be seen in our school shop! A teacher became interested to teach the children to mend. She asked them to bring stockings and other garments from home. Some mothers actually tore holes in old garments and gave them to the children for this purpose! They explained that the garment was useless anyhow and would answer for purposes of learning! The teacher and the children were properly indignant! How can respect for useful work be acquired by doing useless work! Parents often testify to the improved behavior of children at home due to occupations stimulated by the school. This usually occurs when external pressure is removed.

There are no special methods of discipline throughout the school. The children must do as they are told because of their unformed condition, but the school is careful what it tells. Throughout the years we have been accused of conducting a "do as you please school" in spite of the fact that I have repeatedly denied this. Children do not know what is best for them. They have no basis for judgment. They need guidance, control, but this must really be for their good, not merely for the convenience of the adult! Every effort is made to have this conformity merge into and become obedience. That is, to get the child's *will* to act in harmony with the adult will. The fundamental condition for securing the cooperation of the child is to cooperate *with* the child. The teacher, therefore, instinctively grants every request that the children make if it is wholesome and possible to do so. Children should *know* that their wishes are respected by the adult!

Not only is this cooperation with the expressed desire of the child important, but the school endeavors to cooperate in a deeper way with the needs of the child's nature; that is, it aims to anticipate his desires by providing activities and exercises which are in harmony with his stage of development and which will secure the sincerest response.

A "bad" ten-year-old boy came into the school in a sullen, rebellious mood. He found the children engaged in making little caps. "What are they doing?" asked the child. The teacher informed him. "May I make one?" "Certainly," said the teacher. Presently the child was a happy little worker, and was so grateful for the assistance the teacher gave that he cooperated gladly with all of her requests. The cooperative spirit usually accompanies true, wholesome self-expression!

The child must have perfect confidence in the adult. A little boy came into the shop, but hesitated. On being asked if he did not wish to make something, he replied, "Oh, yes,

but I am afraid I might not do it right and then the teacher
will get after me!" "No," was the reply, "the teacher will help
you if you need help." "But," said the child, "I might break
something." "Things do get broken sometimes," said the
teacher "but you need not be afraid of that."

By providing occupations which are creative and which
meet the need of his nature, the child is in the deepest sense
disciplined; that is, he persists and concentrates for things
which he sees to be desirable or necessary. This discipline
gives him the inner satisfaction and consciousness of power
which is the only true reward of all study and work.

Planting Tree in a City Park

6   THE ADOLESCENT

Henderson says: "Children of fifteen who can read, write, and count, and who want to come to the high school, have satisfied the essential requirements for entrance." It will take a long time, no doubt, for general education to accept the idea that the school process should be one of meeting the needs of growth at the various stages of development, rather than making requirements which the children must meet.

The Junior High School movement was instituted to inspire the Grammar School children with the desire for more schooling by giving them a freer, less exacting program during these years. We find that all of our children are keen to go into the high school. We insist that

all children shall be at least fourteen years of age before
entering high school, though some have at times "slipped
through" a little younger.

The atmosphere of the high school is much more
sophisticated than that of the elementary school. The
young people have evening parties and the relation of the
sexes is more conscious. All of this is a forcing process for
younger children. We have tried to have only afternoon or
early evening social functions for the children under
fourteen and we think it would be much better if children of
fourteen and fifteen were protected from the strain of
social stimulation in the high school.

Parents do not yet think of education in terms of growth,
but insist that their children shall be grouped with older
pupils if they can "do the work." In this day when we seem
to be so utterly commercialized, it is very difficult to
persuade parents to give their children more time! The
thought seems to be to hurry them through the high school
and into college as rapidly as possible. Even from the
commercial point of view, it is wiser to prolong childhood.
"My child must earn his living so should get through school
as soon as possible!" Parents should say, "My child must
earn his living, therefore, he must be given ample time for
coordination, integration, and balance. He must have a
broad basis of health and strength to be able to meet the
pressures of our complex civilization!" The student entering college too young profits less by the college experience,
and a very young individual entering professional or
business life is often at a very great disadvantage. Childhood and youth are so short anyhow, and once gone can
never be repeated. Why hurry???

Parents sometimes argue that only the slowly developing
child should be allowed more leisure, that the "precocious"
or rapidly growing individual should be encouraged—yes,
even urged to rush through school. It is difficult to

persuade such parents that the "brilliant" child needs "broadening by retarding," and that here the danger of one-sided development is greater than with the more slowly unfolding organism. So many—in fact, nearly all—of the behavior problems are the result of too much haste in childhood and youth. It is strange that parents do not make positive strenuous efforts to prevent acceleration.

Notwithstanding the fact that all around us are pitiful examples of the unwisdom of haste, parents and many teachers still think it is a credit to the institution and to the family to have children graduate young. "My child graduated from college at twenty and has been an invalid ever since," deplores a mother. "My child went sailing through high school and college, getting honors all the way, and now she has passed away," bemoans a sad father. There is so much testimony against early graduation from college—it is strange that so many parents favor it. A young man who had "finished" college at twenty exclaimed at twenty-two, "Why did my parents and teachers allow it? I ought to be a sophomore right now! I was too young to profit by the college process!" "But", said the mother, "nothing in heaven or earth could have persuaded you at the time to wait even one more year before entering college!" "Yes," replied the youth, "I was determined, as you say, because I knew no better; but if the school had given more creative handwork, music, folk dancing, and sports—I should not have been ready for college until eighteen or nineteen."

Another young man graduating at twenty-three said, "I am sorry I have not another year!" No doubt many real tragedies might be averted by the simple process of prolonging childhood, and giving youth more time."

Excellent scholastic work should be done in the high school, and this requires emphasis upon attainment and achievement. This is the time for strong logical instruction.

This is the time for keen analysis, for following things through, and reasoning things out. The adolescent delights in "doing a piece of work!" There may be danger here of developing self-consciousness, and the student should be protected from this as far as possible, but high school youngsters enjoy *work* as well as play. It is said that the adolescent can work harder, that is, with more spirit and persistence, than at any other time—but should not work under strain because of the great rapidity of growth at this time.

In our high school, homework is assigned and there are examinations, still no child may fail when he does his best. The indications that he is doing his best are: that he attends regularly; that his behavior is acceptable; that he gives reasonable attention to the school work; and that he refrains from all social functions on Monday, Tuesday, Wednesday, and Thursday evenings. The most pronounced phase of growth at this time is —no doubt—social. The social and sex consciousness has arrived and many young people are thrown off their feet, as it were, by this overwhelming development. They are very sensitive to public opinion and special care should be taken to avoid the development of the inferiority complex. The more slowly developing child must be given even greater opportunity for self-expression, and should be encouraged in every way to prevent his being overshadowed by others. It is amazing how some perhaps rather backward students have blossomed in an atmosphere of free, informal discussion rather than the question and answer plan.

In our assignment of homework, we cooperate with the young people by giving no work on Friday, so that they may go home empty-handed with three free evenings to devote to home or social experiences. Then they may return Monday morning "empty-headed" perhaps—but without any feeling of guilt for not having prepared school work.

High school teachers everywhere know very well that children do not study on Friday nights, and neither do they care to study on Saturday, and many parents object to their studying on Sunday—so, the extra tasks that are often assigned on Friday are neglected until perhaps Monday morning and then a great rush is made to do just enough to "get by" in school. The more conscientious pupils deny themselves the social experiences, which may be more important for them than "lessons."

It seems to me that the school, in disregarding the social necessity of these young people, is driving them into underhanded, deceitful attitudes.

Even if their homework has been prepared in the afternoon, we still feel that all high school pupils should remain quietly at home engaging in wholesome, relaxing activity during those four evenings each week. Parents often do not realize that an evening of excitement at the theater or at a party has a very disconcerting effect on the work of the school the next day, even though all assignments have been prepared! It has been difficult to get some parents to cooperate with us in keeping the young people quiet four evenings each week, though there is an increasing tendency to do so. American home-life might, to a certain degree, be restored if parents and teachers could unite to reserve four evenings each week to study, conversation, singing, or playing games in the home.

Of course, exceptions may be made—but in order to have serious, earnest work in the high school, we feel that these four evenings should be spent quietly.

The examinations which the teachers sometimes give are in no sense designed to find out whether the pupils should remain in their group; they are not given in order to find out whether the children are ready to pass, nor even to measure specific knowledge. They are quite valuable, however, in helping the teacher to realize how the work has been presented and grasped. Sometimes in these examinations books may be used, to see if they are able to find their way easily. Often the questions are merely thought provoking. They also help the student to know whether his effort has been well or mis-directed. The students are now conscious of the value of concentrated study and understand the reasonableness of requirements and should cooperate heartily with the teacher. A spirit of evasion, or an effort to appear to know when he does not—an inclination to try to "get by"—should be unknown in the high school, and constitute a real problem when present.

All classes in the high school are organized and are free to originate and carry through projects in connection with the regular school work. The captain of the girls' basketball team planned money-raising schemes to provide the means to take the team to a neighboring school for a game! Some of the teachers complained of "neglect of school work." They failed to recognize that real power was being developed. It is very difficult for teachers to feel that a social experience of that kind has as great if not greater educational value than class room work. When this girl later achieved distinction because of presence of mind, self-control, courage, and common sense, some were convinced, but others still doubted! Will the teaching profession ever develop the ability to recognize human power as the chief aim in education?

A social committee from the faculty is appointed to cooperate with the students, sometimes taking the initiative in devising social functions. The folk dance is emphasized in the high school and many social events grow out of this form of expression. A folk dancing party is given once a month and one evening a week a folk dancing class is offered for those who would like more work than the school affords. A number of our high school graduates were invited to dance in the English Village at the World's Fair in

Chicago, and again in San Diego, Cleveland, and Dallas. "It is wonderful," wrote one girl, "to be paid for having such a good time!" It was most thrilling for these young people to be employed as professional dancers when they had no special training, other than the regular class work in the high school. A school bus was donated and the teacher of folk dancing made many trips to neighboring cities demonstrating the Old English Country and Morris dances. Every class claims the privilege of a number of week-end hikes during the year, besides time given for camping. We consider these experiences highly educational. The art of living together for a few days, of preparing food, of using the time to advantage, of adjusting to one another, is most important. Of course, adults always accompany them, the children choosing the chaperones. Sometimes complaints have been made of the behavior of new pupils, but those who have learned how to use liberty are usually very reliable.

The school day closes at three o'clock, which gives time for athletics. Both boys and girls organize basketball teams and the boys engage in football and baseball. The tennis court is in constant requisition. Volleyball and barn ball are often enjoyed. Being so close to the Bay, swimming is a great attraction. Dramatics are a great means of education and are used constantly by all groups. Many simple one-act plays are given before the group, then perhaps repeated before the whole school. Often these plays are given before other groups such as P.T.A. Meetings, or other social gatherings. Once or twice a year each class gives a performance in the public hall, sometimes even charging an admission fee. The high school children get the greatest pleasure in selecting a play, often taking the lead and sometimes rejecting the teacher's counsel. However, in most cases they are perfectly willing to be guided. The teacher often insists, however, that the pupils "did it all themselves" and this is quite evident from the enthusiasm of the children. We have always endeavored to avoid what is known as a "play producer." We feel that dramatics should grow out of the school work as fully as possible and should be directed and presented by the teacher in charge, rather than by a professional. Professionals always concentrate their attention upon the production. Emphasis should always be upon the effect of the performance on the children, not upon the perfection of the production!

I have witnessed many performances by high school students in which the hand of the "producer" quite overshadowed the individual performer. Not only is the theme and content often quite beyond the grasp of the children, but there is a lamentable lack of spontaneity and self-expression. Children should *enjoy* the rehearsals and there should never be any strain or exhaustion in giving the play. There is no greater socializing experience than that found in dramatics of the right sort. The complete development of the social impulse is the highest in man. Why should not the schools offer the fullest opportunity for the growth of the great art of human relations in dramatics, handwork, community singing, folk dancing, and sports? Throughout our high school, just as in the lower school, our aim is constantly to evaluate all work by its *effect on the children* rather than by the external result of attainment or achievement.

Work in the craft room and the shop continues in the high school, often with even greater vigor and enthusiasm than shown by the younger children. One period of shop is substituted by work in the science laboratory for the higher classes. The corner of the shop where work in silver, brass, and copper is offered, is the center of the most stimulating and delightful activity. This is the time for the development of ideals and standards.

The ambition and desire of the children to do this work is limited only to their ability to pay for the material. They not only undertake trays and vases, but go in for bracelets, pins, and rings and aspire to the setting of precious stones. The work in pottery and clay modeling still attracts; and in weaving, some very interesting rugs and baskets have been produced. The high school children enjoy making furniture, the girls often turning out as well finished articles as the boys. We consider our shop the most important place on the campus. While attention is given to technique, greater attention is given to the effect of this work on the pupil. Many a trifling, indifferent student has made remarkable strides in concentration, seriousness, and devotion to school work through power developed here. The town is filled with articles produced in the school shop. All pupils work in the shop one or two periods every day—and it is the most inspiring sight to see from twenty to fifty children and young people in deepest concentration happily occupied at self-initiated tasks! Some of our students have been able to earn a part of college expenses by their ability to assist in crafts.

There are many problems of discipline in the high school. Parents who are not thoughtful, who leave all for teachers to manage, who often allow pupils to participate in unwholesome experiences, often find their children becoming more and more difficult and sometimes feel obligated to take their children out of school, always blaming the teacher. These problems however, do not usually arise at times when the work is creative. Of course, the temperament, personality, and wisdom of the teacher are always involved in behavior problems. Many high school teachers and college professors fail to realize that they are often personally responsible for failures in scholarship and behavior even in college!

The registrar reporting poor work of a college student admitted that the instructor was "difficult." Teachers are usually "difficult" when obliged to meet external standards, making their work more rigid and mechanical than human.

A young college boy exclaimed, "Professor ——— ought to be shot! He is mean, sarcastic, and he doesn't *care* whether we get anything or not!"

An effort is made to have as much of the work as possible creative. Academic work may be creative in large measure, but there are phases in which it is more or less routine and requires concentration and perseverance that some young people are not quite able to give. There are no rules that children may break. A few simple requirements are necessary, but these are usually recognized as reasonable and, in the main, the young people cooperate with the school quite heartily. We have never been able to develop an interest in self-government and have never felt the necessity. I have always doubted the wisdom of "self-government" in high schools. All real government rests on force. Children should not have the experience of *controlling* others! Impersonal judgment is an attainment not always reached by adults. Penalties should never be imposed by children. It tends to develop self-righteousness, egotism, and priggishness.

There is no "passing grade." Here in the high school, as in the lower school, no child may fail. In cases of an undeveloped condition more time may be necessary, but this is in no sense considered a failure nor is a decision to require more time reached by any form of examination.

The one thing required of all children in the high school is that they do their best. Of course, this best is largely the result of the kind of work presented and the manner of presentation by the teacher. Instead of the standard of a general idea of what may be expected of the average child, the teacher should develop a keen and definite judgment of individual ability and endeavor to keep each pupil up to this standard. This may be determined by the manner in which the student attacks the work, and the evident resulting satisfaction. We believe that all children do their best when they are interested, so the great problem is to stimulate and preserve this fundamental interest. We believe that the mind is normally interested in mathematics. It is true, however, that some minds do not respond readily to the higher forms of mathematics. "I don't want to study algebra," exclaims a fourteen-year-old—"and I'm not going to college!" "Very well," replies the teacher. "Are you willing to attend the class doing the best you can?" "Yes, I don't mind that." At the end of the year, this student moved away, entering a conventional school, and was given full "credit" for a year of algebra! In such cases, it often pays to be quite frank with the young people and tell them that this necessity is made by the very unwise college entrance requirements. Since these requirements exist and the child wishes to go to college, then we urge him to concentrate his attention to the best of his ability, being assured that if this is done—he cannot fail.

The time will no doubt soon arrive when the only requirements for college entrance will be:

That the student is eighteen years of age or older; that at least some time has been spent in profitable, intellectual work; and that the student himself desires to attend. This will come when the college becomes the conscious agent of progress and accepts its responsibility—that of ministering to the young adult. The questions then asked the candidate for admission will be merely: What do you want—what do you need?? And the nature of growth, the special needs and interests of the individual, will indicate the answer.

There is no doubt real value to every individual in the study of algebra and geometry, but certainly not enough to make it the condition of further study in other directions. But I believe every normal young person would very willingly and sincerely engage in the study of higher mathematics—if he were allowed to progress at his own pace and were not obliged to reach any fixed external standard! One period daily for a year or two might be very profitable and happily spent under the mental stimulus of problems in higher mathematics—and in some cases the experience might be so thrilling and delightful that further study would be desired. But the student should never feel the burden of forced continuation of such work.

Sometimes parents encourage their children to believe that there is "no use" in the study of Latin. They are quite right, I believe, in feeling that to be *obliged* to master any particular amount of Latin is unnecessary. When the children see the value of studying the meanings of words and if the work is presented without too much emphasis upon grammar, being careful not to be too exacting, we find that most all children are happy and eager to enter this new field. Word analysis is valuable and an excellent substitute for Latin. It is difficult, however, to find teachers able to vitalize this work. If conversations are undertaken in this language and brief dramatic performances occasionally given, real joy in mastery is experienced. We give two years of Latin and no child may fail if he does anywhere near his best. This is indicated by attack of the subject and absorption in it. The teacher uses his own method in this as in all teaching. We have no "method"—no "system"—but are working from the point of view of the development of childhood and youth, rather than the development of "subject matter." The student is not obliged to reach any degree of efficiency in the subject, but we do insist all the way along that his effort is sincere. Cases of trifling in this school, as in all others, are treated as particular personal problems. We cannot claim freedom from such problems but all of the teachers testify that there are fewer here than in most high schools.

Every mind is thrilled by the study of science. We believe that the children in the elementary school need nature study and that the children of the high school should have four years of science. When it is presented in a simple, human way and no external demands or requirements made for passing, we find nearly all pupils taking a very keen delight in the subject. This work enlarges one's consciousness of the universe. One young high school boy exclaimed, "Oh, mother, I never dreamed anything could be so wonderful as physics!"

It is creative in the best sense and will, no doubt, furnish delightful intellectual occupation for leisure time. It has always been a mystery to me that so many children who are very eager and keen in their study of science in the high school, are repelled by the uninteresting and stern demands of science work in college. This seems quite tragical and I am sure if the instructors in the college would study the development of the child and get at the subject from the student's point of view, this tragedy might be avoided. Sometimes in the high school the teacher introduces so many formulae, so much mathematics in the work in science, that some young people, especially girls, are repelled. All teachers should bear in mind constantly that the subject matter mastered is not as important as the stimulation of thought, the joy and satisfaction of the student.

"Who determines your course of study?" asked a mother of the science professor in the university. "I do," replied the bland instructor. "Well," continued the mother, "you have been teaching this subject many years and science has revealed her secrets to you. When you arrange the course for these young, undeveloped seventeen- and eighteen-year-old boys and girls fresh from the village high schools, do you select the wonderful things of science that will attract and thrill them, making an indelible impression upon them and permanently enriching their lives, even if they remain only a few months? Or, do you emphasize the technically logical sequences which will prepare them to become specialists as you are?" After thinking a moment the professor admitted, "Yes, I fear we are too technical."

General science, biology and botany, physics and chemistry are offered in our high school. We believe science is truly "cultural" and should be a source of delight throughout one's entire life.

History is another subject which is highly stimulating and delightful. It is remarkable that history, which is the story of mankind, should repel so many young people. I feel certain that this is due in the main to the college entrance requirements. A college professor of history conducted the work as a "story hour." The interest and enthusiasm of those college students was amazing. A number of them became so absorbed that they acquired a private historical library and became life-long students. All were awakened to the importance of historical knowledge in gaining an understanding of modern life. High school teachers, feeling the demand for thoroughness not only in understanding causes and sequences, but the memorizing of events, dates, etc., continue to harass many young people. The instructors think that students should *master* the subject; whereas, the important thing is that a *love* for the subject be developed. We give our high school students four years of history, although perhaps all of this is not absolutely required for college entrance. We believe, however, that history is so developing, so stimulating, so invaluable to all thinking, that children of this age should not be denied the enrichment of mind which it affords.

If history stories are enjoyed during the school days, no doubt a taste for historical movement may be developed which might save many minds from the perversion of undesirable fiction. We contend that high school work is *not* a preparation for college, but the satisfying of a present need. Surely the young need to experience the thrill of a great historical drama.

Students who have four years of wholesome, happy, and intelligent work and study *are* ready for the next process! Since no student is required to attain any particular degree of excellence, both teachers and pupils may concentrate with abandon upon the topic in hand. Teachers in the conventional school often complain that the necessity for "covering the ground" prevents the fullest understanding and enjoyment of the work. Henderson says that history should never be studied or "learned," but read and enjoyed. By making no definite requirements for passing, we find our children sincerely interested in all matters of human import.

Of course, the high school pupil should study English during the whole four years. If there is any one subject in the world that should be delightful, it is English. To read poetry and stories and other delightful pieces of literature and discuss them; to write freely in response to one's desire to express; yes, and occasionally to analyze the language is thrilling even to a slow mind. But to be marked and graded on the *form* one uses in expressing matters of vital interest is to drive back the creative flow of thought, imagination, and expression.

A college professor marked a student "failed" because his very clever poem, enjoyed by the entire class, had faults of punctuation and spelling! Of course, that student never ventured again to write with abandon. This is why children are so often hesitant in class, though talkative enough outside the school! "English is very hard and uninteresting," complain many freshmen in college. "We should have been better prepared in high school!" No one will ever know how much beauty of expression, and perhaps of life, has been checked or destroyed by the criticism of well-intentioned instructors! The humiliation a child may suffer when his sincere effort is rejected on account of form is unpleasant to contemplate. "But," exclaims the conserva-

tive, "will you permit all sorts of errors?" Certainly not, but
the atmosphere of the classroom must be sympathetic
enough for students to express themselves freely, and be
able to accept correction and suggestion without being
inhibited. This is the art of the teacher, and this would no
doubt be constantly in evidence if the teacher were free!
The chilled, dead souls of the adult world bear constant
witness to the evil effect of the wrong point of view in the
teaching of English. "A student may have *nothing* worth
saying, but if the form is correct his work is acceptable; he
may have the finest possible thought but if the form is
faulty, his work is rejected," explained a serious-minded
professor of English!

We should never forget that language is a tool to be used
only when there are thoughts pressing for utterance! It is
tragedy to have thought destroyed by self-consciousness
caused by criticism. I believe children love to write. Who
dares deny his early aspirations! Even to become a poet!

Of course, dramatics grow out of the work in English to a
large extent. Children of high school years should be keenly
interested in grammar and rhetoric, also. However, this is
where most teachers fail and young people lose interest.
They try too hard to make the pupils thorough! There is
not enough relaxation, not enough interest. I wonder if the
work of grammar and rhetoric should not be postponed
until the college level! College professors constantly find
fault with what has been taught in the high school. They
seem to enjoy "flunking" the pupils in English. Much more
time should be devoted to reading and enjoying the classics
than to the analysis of construction. Too much time is spent
in studying about literature, not enough in its enjoyment.

We are making a great effort to make the study of English
a tool which may be used properly for the expression of
ideas. The emphasis, then, would be put upon the idea to be
expressed—not merely the form in which it appears. When

thinking is in progress and children feel free to express themselves without fear of criticism, a power of expression is developed which welcomes suggestion. A college professor allowed his pupils great freedom of expression, the result being productions of literary value, and consequent health of spirit for the students. All "help" offered by teachers which dulls the desire to express, is not help, but obstruction. The thousands of "mute and inglorious Miltons" no doubt are due to early repression caused by self-consciousness as a result of criticism.

The pupils in the high school are eager to publish a paper, they are interested to write letters. Theme writing often becomes a matter of great enthusiasm and satisfaction. When this is not true, the teacher should examine himself and his method. We must never forget that the adolescent period is a very wobbly, uncertain time in the life of the human being. We need not expect mature responsibility, nor compelling aim, nor fully controlled desires. To see young people supremely absorbed in any wholesome interest is one of the greatest rewards.

Every teacher in the high school should study this period of adolescence with an open mind and should constantly check his impulse to criticize, dominate, and condemn by a deeper knowledge of the particular stage in which these young people are. Some critics insist that the very best teaching is done in the kindergarten and the worst in the college. The kindergartners and the elementary school teachers are trained to respect growth and to provide the right conditions for childhood; whereas, in the high schools and colleges the main emphasis is upon the mastering of subject matter, and teachers are constantly criticizing the work of the student rather than judging their own ability to instruct.

A college professor once declared, "Latin may be taught by any old tintype!" College entrance requirements con-

tinue to handicap teachers and inhibit students. This often
repels the young, sometimes to the point of resistance.
Then we hear teachers bemoaning the fact that "children
will *not* study unless forced to do so!" The high school and
college teachers are burdened with external standards. A
certain more human college professor, in a confidential talk
with a student, explained how he was bound by the college
authorities! This professor was apologetic because of his
own unsympathetic attitude and explained that he worked
"under pressure!" Many have not the slightest glimpse of
an inner standard. This must be developed. May we ever
hope for this while there are college entrance requirements? We are defeating our own ends. English, including
literature, the most spiritually inspiring of all studies, the
study that should be pursued with great joy, affording
permanent satisfactions, often becomes wooden and
mechanical. And this is the consequence of the absolutely
unnecessary, illogical, and inhuman college entrance examinations! "What a delight it would be for us all if we could
take more time to enjoy these selections of prose and
poetry," bemoaned a high school teacher. "But we must
'cover certain ground' or these students will not be accepted
in college".

Our program then in the high school consists of four
years of just as serious and earnest work as we can persuade
the young people to do—in science, history, and at least two
years of mathematics and language—which may be substituted part of the time by social studies, such as civics,
problems of democracy, or economics.

The children are always keen to enter upon the study of
French. They feel the vitality and reality of studying a living
language. Conversational French is used largely—even in
the high school—though attention is given to reading,
grammar, and composition. Arts and crafts, woodworking,

dramatics, folk dancing and singing, and sports are important parts of the curriculum of the high school.

The school day is three hours and a half in the morning and an hour and a half in the afternoon, giving plenty of time for sports, recreation, and relaxation at the noon hour. We value "sound scholarship"—we aim to develop concentration and perseverance. We believe that high school students should develop mental grasp and grow in self-control and ideals.

We believe that the high school would be better able to attain these ends if there were no entrance requirements into college, and we insist that after four years of study, work, and play under the direction, stimulation, and instruction of earnest, able, consecrated adults, the young people *are* ready for the next—the college process—and we say to the colleges, "Here they are—take them and lead them into a larger life." Our graduates have entered many colleges on certificate and have done well.

English Folk Dance Demonstration

7 THE YOUNG ADULT

From the point of view that education is a preparation for vocations or for adult life, there may be many young people who are not "college material." From the point of view that education is life—growth—all normal young people are "college material." Society must minister to all the children of all the people throughout the growing years. The college attitude is too often that of having a certain definite something to offer and insisting that the young people be "prepared" to accept this offering, or as they often express it, "profit by the college experience." And after the student has been admitted into the college, he is often dismissed because he is unable to reach a certain scholastic standard. "No matter how earnest and faithful a student is, if he cannot reach this particular grade, he is wasting his time and his father's money," explained a college official. This ignores the social value of the college life and the mental grasp that may be developing. "I insist," said one college professor, "that the college has the right to decide, not only what subjects are taught in the high school, but also what pupils are prepared to take what we have to give!" All "requirements" should come from below rather than settled in advance. What is being done now should determine the next step. The needs of the children in the grammar school should suggest the high school process, and the high school should indicate what the college should offer! But the college claims that it is the business of the elementary and high school to *prepare* the pupils, and that the college is free to accept or reject them. This is eminently unfair from every angle. The school can never know exactly what the college demands, and can never be quite certain that the students are really prepared to meet these. "These are fine young people with excellent minds, but they have not had the exact preparation," explained an instructor in a great college. The demands naturally change and should change in a growing society, but fundamentally the college should not make demands, but strive to *meet* the demands of youth.

From the point of view that education is life—growth —and not a preparation, it follows that the school program must be a life-giving process for the little child, a life-giving process for the young people, and a life-giving process for the young college student. This assumes that the school and college programs are merely means for providing conditions for growth at the different levels, and that the door is open all the way!

The greatest concern of the college would then be to meet the needs of youth. It is amazing to note what life sometimes does for the young! High school students who are the despair of their elders often return after a year or two, earnest, reliable, upstanding, full of hope and confidence. The child is unformed, unripe, immature, ignorant. He is a victim of the conditions which the adult provides. Youth has not yet come into full self-direction and control, is not yet in full possession of its power. This puts upon society the tremendous responsibility of providing for childhood, youth, and the young adult right conditions for continuing growth.

The college must change its point of view. It must accept wholeheartedly its responsibility to society. If this were done, the high school would be free, and also the lower school, from all external demands, and teachers could then live with their students in a direct, vital way. The colleges need not fear to receive all young people—for they would find a finer and finer quality of high school graduates knocking at their doors. "I cannot begin to express the joy I feel in the frank, happy, unself-conscious response of these youngsters," said a teacher of wide experience, but new in our school. The elementary and high school could frankly study the need of the growing organism and make a sincere effort to meet that need. This would make the work of teaching so thrilling, so creative, that many more able minds would be attracted to the profession.

Self-consciousness might be prevented and there need be no inferiority complex, no fear of failure. The children and young people would grow clear-eyed and steady-nerved. There need be no reason for "trying to get by." There would be no flunking, no examinations for which to cram, no spasmodic concentration followed by languor or dissipation. The college doors would thus be open to all normal young people of eighteen years of age or older. In case of over-crowding, the preference might be given to those who have had four years of the high school process, but many new colleges would spring up in response to this demand.

Since the young people are not yet fully coordinated and integrated, they would need guidance and control. The fundamental condition for growth at this level is social; the colleges might well insist on giving all students experiences in those activities which are intrinsically social, such as dramatics, sports, community singing, dancing, and all forms of the arts. Then the other courses might be selected by preference of the student. No doubt the student will need the guidance of high school instructors, parents, and college counsellors in choosing courses. If the proper spirit prevailed in the college, students would never be tempted to select "snap courses" but would enter upon the work with eagerness and confidence. Specialization, "pre-requisite" courses for professions, should properly begin at twenty-one or twenty-two—certainly not until the third or fourth year of college. Even here, there is great complaint of inflexibility and unreasonableness in college requirements. Our whole educational system, cultural and professional, is too fixed, wooden, sadly in need of humanizing.

The testimony of wise observers supports the idea that those students whose work up to twenty-one or twenty-two has not been in connection with any vocation but rather for the purpose of "awakening, enlightening, and enlivening the mind" have become superior workers in any profession. Immediate intellectual joy and satisfaction are much more developing because more direct and sincere, and this must necessarily result in a higher efficiency.

I feel certain that if the colleges could trust the mind they would find that, at this age, young people love to study and love to work, and want to know. They love philosophy, history, science, sociology, and many aspiring young people are eager for the most challenging intellectual activity. "What can be done!" exclaimed a despairing professor. "The young men care for nothing but joy-riding, parties, etc." "I am not so sure of that," replied a business man. "A number of your students visited my office the other afternoon and we all nearly missed dinner, so absorbing was the conversation on the philosophy of Kant!" "I wonder," queried the professor, "if we are working from the wrong point of view!" All young people are keenly interested in the meaning of life and things, but usually hesitate when this work is demanded or made a condition for success or graduation!

The prolonging of childhood is still the hope of the race. Specialization always tends to crystallization. Care should be taken to avoid overspecialization, at any age.

The time is not far distant when society will provide for all young—guidance and control, instruction, stimulation, association, and inspiration throughout the growing years until the physical growth has been attained at about twenty-two or twenty-three years of age—or, as Dewey says, until they are ready to control and direct their own careers. They will then be ready to make their contribution to society. There will always be opportunity for them to go back to college from time to time for special six weeks', three months'—or whole year courses as desired in any particular subject. A young man who had enjoyed college, graduated with honors and was interested to continue study, said, "I never again will study anything anywhere if I am subject to examination or grading!" A young woman, Phi Beta Kappa, exclaimed, "I cannot tell you how *glad* I am, how free and relieved and happy to know, I shall never again have to take an examination!"

The American Folk School, patterned after the Danish School, is no doubt destined to have a very great influence on American adult education. This school has no requirements for entrance except "suitable maturity," and no requirements for continuance or exit. There are no records, nor grades, nor diplomas. The time is spent in a most interesting, profitable way in lectures and the discussion of topics of interest, singing, dancing, nature studies, arts and crafts, and other social experiences. How may we ever acquire the one great art, the all comprehensive, all including art of human relations, unless the schools and colleges provide fullest opportunity humanly to relate! Life is growth. Growth waits upon renewal of mind. Education must come into its own. It must become the conscious agent for building a better world. It must be true to its high mission. Its responsibility is to see to it that the child and youth grow in such a way that their minds may be forever and constantly renewed. The greatest tragedy that can come to anyone is to lose interest in the new, the ever enlarging of experience. Arrest of development or crystallization, which is now so apt to be the result of our educational process, should be unknown. If college entrance requirements were removed, there would be freedom all along the line, and the school would be free to provide conditions which would prevent arrest of development. Examinations in the college should be conducted merely for the purpose of helping the student and the instructor to understand more fully the quality of the work. This does not refer to technical, professional work. Of course, no one should be allowed to enter the professions without thorough preparation, but this should not interfere with growth during the early years, nor should it prevent or obstruct cultural development in the college. There should be no external standard for promotion or graduation. There should be no failures in colleges as there are no failures in the lower school. There will be no "courses" to complete—but merely topics of interest or subjects to study, and these will be selected by the students—under proper advice.

A degree is medieval and does not belong to education. No one should ever study for a degree. The only reward for study is knowing, and the fact that a student has been in attendance at a creditable institution should be sufficient guarantee. Education must move out and away from commercialism. All true education is intrinsically vocational.

The finest development of the individual is the truest education, and this development is the best preparation for any vocation excepting necessary technical information or skill. There are many people with high degrees who are inefficient in service and lacking in social qualitites.

"Are all the people worthy to whom you grant degrees?" a registrar was asked.

"No, indeed," was the reply.

"Well, then," responded the questioner, "since degrees are given to unworthy people, which at least partially destroys their value, why give degrees at all? Would not a statement of attendance answer the purpose?"

Since the degree is so meaningless, why should we preserve it? Education must be free from the inhibiting, stultifying, death-giving atmosphere of medieval scholasticism.

Mrs. Johnson Conducting Training Session

8 TEACHERS TRAINING

Now a word about teachers training: The three fundamental requisites for all teachers are that they love, understand, and are sincerely interested in children; second, that they have sufficient scholarship; and third, that they are interested in all matters of social welfare.

This requires an open-minded, earnest study of the development of the child. This study can never be finished. Probably no one will ever be able to say, "I know all about the nature and need of childhood—and am able to meet these needs." This is the teacher's task, nevertheless.

There are two ways of doing this: One is to study the findings of the great psychologists and students of child growth. The other is to watch the reaction of the child and to know whether this reaction is desirable or undesirable.

Every teacher should be able to go into any school room anywhere and, after a few moments' observation, know whether the children are languishing or flourishing—and why. She should know whether the nervous system is being violated—whether or not the children are being accelerated or subjected to severe forms of specialization. She should be able to detect external pressure, self-consciousness, any other unwholesome condition. This is a very desirable accomplishment for all adults. We do not know how to observe. We have no standard of judgment. If the children appear to be well and happy and seem to enjoy the work, we think they are flourishing—even when the work is really quite unsuitable for them.

We need not repeat nor emphasize that it is obviously necessary for teachers to be well informed. Not only should they have had the work usually offered in the elementary, high school, and college curricula, they should be earnest students of life and progress. Beside this, however, I believe the elementary teacher should have had, in her own experience, the things through which childhood must develop.

All children need music—that is, singing, dancing, rhythm, and dramatics. All children need handwork. All children need nature and stories and play. Therefore, the teacher of primary and elementary grades should have had much experience in all these lines of educational activity, that she may be able to provide right conditions for children and to help them attain their ends.

How could it be possible for a teacher to guide children adequately if she had never known the delight of work in clay, painting, drawing, wood and leather and all other craft materials? How can she be "fit to live with children" if she knows nothing and does not care for all the things in nature? All teachers in training should have experience in nature, crafts, and folk dancing.

In the high school where departmental instruction is given, it is necessary for the teacher not only to "know her subject" but to know adolescence and to be in full sympathy with the nature of growth at this stage. It is infinitely more important that a child shall love and enjoy geometry than that he rank high in attainment or achievement. It is vital for young people to enjoy literature, to be thrilled by the work in English. This is much more necessary to their growth and welfare than for them to be able to pass informational tests.

It is profoundly necessary for the teacher in the high school to be able to recognize the value of social relations in a camping trip, a project, a party, a dramatic performance. She must understand and sympathize with the attraction between John and Mary. She should be a competent and desirable chaperone at social functions, and her work in the high school should preserve—not destroy—her power that she may enter into the young people's pleasures with enthusiasm. These, the well-qualified teacher of the adolescent will be able to evaluate truly. The time may come when the college extra-curricular activities will be ranked as being of as great value as any classroom study.

The folk dance lends itself particularly to the social development of the adolescent and young adult—that is, for the high school and college process. The folk dance is rhythmical, it is objective, thus preventing self-consciousness, and every movement is for some definite purpose. It requires no special costume. It is highly social. It is impossible for young people to engage in the folk dance for any length of time without becoming conscious of an inner center to which the rest of the body relates. They also become conscious of a very beautiful form being expressed of which they are a part. Too often, in our high schools and colleges young people become more and more individualized or arrested in their social development by the consciousness of demands by the institution. The fear of failure—or the triumph of success—is a very individual affair. The natural development is toward a more socialized, impersonal, unselfish attitude. The self-consciousness resulting from the demands of the system prevents this and we find many very intellectual people, with high scholastic records, quite undeveloped socially. The teacher must understand and value all socializing influences, and strive to provide conditions for the finest development of a social spirit in the students. All teachers should also take a deep and active interest in all social or economic problems. They should develop the alert mind, earnestly striving to understand human motives and forces. They should not be afraid to face, understand, and cooperate with efforts toward a better social order. Teachers should never forget that they are citizens and under obligations to use whatever influence they may have for the betterment of society—as well as to provide conditions for the young to develop into open-minded citizens. They should not only strive to vote intelligently but should be able to avoid narrow partisanship. In a changing world, the finest influence the high school pupil can have is that of a teacher unafraid of change, open-minded, with an understanding confidence and an earnest desire to cooperate with those who would correct social evils in a sane, controlled manner. In other words, a teacher should believe in peaceful evolution—never in violent revolution—and young people should be helped to understand that inquiry, investigation, and hearty peaceful cooperation are the only safe methods. Teachers, however, cannot be ignorant of—nor indifferent to social wrong or injustice —and young people should develop a sensitiveness that impels them ever to work earnestly for right human relations. If young people are to escape prejudice and intolerance, they must have tolerant, sympathetic, understanding teachers.

There is needed a unit experiment beginning with the nursery school and extending through the college process without "let or hindrance." This means no entrance examinations at any time. The school process would be that of frankly ministering to the young at each stage of development. There would be guidance and control—but no inhibiting self-consciousness, no doubt of motives, no fundamental insincerity. The adults would concentrate upon the nature and the need of childhood and youth, providing activities and exercises which minister to the all-round health of the body, to the development of mental grasp, and preserving the sincerity and unself-consciousness of the emotional life. The degree or diploma would merely mark the close of the process and would not in any way indicate the quality of work done. The end would be immediate—that is, the school would accept the responsibility of making the experience valuable—resting assured that a well-spent today is the best preparation for tomorrow.

In this unit experiment there might be developed the finest sort of teachers' training process. The primary, elementary, and high school groups could be used as a laboratory for practice teaching. Here prospective teachers would have an opportunity to work with children from the point of view of their nature and need, and not be hampered by the demands of the system. Too often, in training schools the student studies the development of the child, but is obliged to teach according to the curriculum.

There would be no teaching of subjects nor teaching of children. The effort would be to provide experiences and studies through which childhood and youth develop. Development—growth—would be the immediate end. Many teachers deny that they teach subjects, declaring that they teach the children. The time will soon come when they will insist that their sole aim is to provide the conditions of growth, using certain subjects and activities as means only.

The course of study for teachers in training then must necessarily include singing, folk dancing, dramatics, nature, arts and crafts, woodworking, story telling, and sports. Practice teaching and the study of the development of the child are of supreme importance—and psychology and history of education might profitably be added. An intelligent teacher is always able to produce subject matter, but sometimes long experience is necessary to equip one with the ability to provide the right conditions of growth and to detect the signs of wholesomeness.

If such a project could be conducted for twenty or more years, it might have a profound influence in changing the point of view of general education. To see young people emerging from a school process free from external standards, meeting life satisfactorily, would be convincing—and certainly the teaching profession would rejoice to be free from all the grading, reports, records, and the heartbreaking experience of having to "fail" pupils.

Modern courses of study have been outlined. Almost perfect methods have been developed, but there is yet to emerge the inner standard which must eventually prevail. It is that standard which identifies growth with education. It is a standard which the institution must meet. It depends upon a thorough and increasing knowledge of the nature and needs of childhood and youth, and a profound conviction that supplying these needs is the one and only essential.

It is very thrilling to contemplate what society might be in a few years if our educational system could accept and apply this point of view. No examinations—no tests—no failures—no rewards—no self-consciousness; the development of sincerity, the freedom of children to live their lives straight out—no double motives—children never subjected to the temptation to cheat—even to appear to know when they do not know; the development of fundamental sincerity, which is the basis of all morality.

Said a visiting relative of a child: "Of course, I know she has not acquired the knowledge of subject matter she would have gotten in the conventional school, but she has gained something of infinitely greater value."

This child had been greatly accelerated and through self-consciousness had lost childhood's charm. She gradually lost some of her sophistication and recovered some charm.

Some one queried: "How do you *know* she has not acquired the usual subject matter?"

"Why, I don't know—but I suppose I judged this because of the absence of a report card!"

I suppose most adults judge the progress of children by the report cards. One father, however, bemoaned the fact that his daughter had gone clear through high school without being touched by the process.

The development of the open mind—that is, the ability to wait for data—is most important. The development of power to find out what is true and take *it* for authority —rather than hastily taking truth on authority.

Think what all this would do for the teaching profession! The work of all teachers would become creative in the finest sense. At the close of the day, the teacher might well ask herself these questions: Was the work done today, wholesome and interesting? Was the order of the development of the nervous system respected? Was there growth in mental grasp? Was the sincerity and unself-consciousness of the emotional life preserved?

They would learn to watch the development of children and youth—they would become expert in evaluating extra-curricular activities. There would be no soft indulgence. Even the sternest control and direction would be necessary. Trifling would not be allowed.

All ends would be immediate. The process and the end are one. Concentrated effort with resulting satisfactions would be the end desired, rather than attainment and achievement, although attainment and achievement must necessarily accompany such effort.

Young people would move joyously on, never knowing failure, overcoming discouragement, never acquiring the inferiority complex, never experiencing a broken body caused by meeting school requirements. Youth would emerge from the college process clear-eyed, steady-nerved, clean-blooded, with confidence in themselves and the universe, ready to meet whatever life has to offer, with the certainty which consciousness of power and sincerity of purpose give. True discipline results in a knowledge of law in themselves and the universe which they gladly obey!

"It doth not yet appear what we shall be." It is the work of education to assist the self-realization of every human being. Education must lead society. Education's responsibility is that of building a better world. Education must become a vital force in the modeling of our economic and social structure. Education cannot repudiate its responsibility. It dare not fail.

APPENDIX
AN EXCERPT FROM
"SCHOOLS OF TOMORROW"
BY JOHN AND EVELYN DEWEY

John Dewey, internationally famed as a philosopher and educator, regarded Marietta Johnson's work with total enthusiasm, and helped to make her activities known both at home and abroad. The following excerpt from the book Schools of Tomorrow, *by John and Evelyn Dewey, copyright 1915 by E. P. Dutton & Co. Inc. Renewal, 1943 by John Dewey and Evelyn Dewey. © Renewal 1962 by E. P. Dutton & Co. Inc. Used with their permission.*

Rousseau's teaching that education is a process of natural growth has influenced most theorizing upon education since his time. It has influenced the practical details of school work to a less degree. Occasionally, however, experimenters have based their plans upon his principles.

Among these experiments is one conducted by Mrs. Johnson at Fairhope, Alabama. To this spot during the past few years students and experts have made pilgrimages, and the influence of Mrs. Johnson's model has led to the starting of similar schools in different parts of the United States. Mrs. Johnson carries on a summer course for training teachers by giving a working object lesson in her ideas at Greenwich, Connecticut, where a school for children has been conducted as a model.

Her main underlying principle is Rousseau's central idea, namely: The child is best prepared for life as an adult by experiencing in childhood what has meaning to him as a child; and, further, the child has a right to enjoy his childhood. Because he is a growing animal who must develop so as to live successfully in the grown-up world, nothing should be done to interfere with growth, and everything should be done to further the full and free development of his body and his mind. These two developments go on together; they are inseparable processes and must both be constantly borne in mind as of equal importance.

Mrs. Johnson criticizes the conventional school of today. She says it is arranged to make things easy for the teacher who wishes quick and tangible results; that it disregards the full development of the pupils. It is arranged on the fatal plan of a hothouse, forcing to a sterile show, rather than fostering all-around growth. It does not foster an individuality capable of an enduring resistance and of creative activities. It disregards the *present* needs of the child; the fact that he is living a full life each year and hour, not waiting to live in some period defined by his elders, when school is a thing of the past. The distaste of children for school is a natural and necessary result of such mistakes as these. Nature has not adapted the young animal to the narrow desk, the crowded curriculum, the silent absorption of complicated facts. His very life and growth depend upon motion, yet the school forces him into a cramped position for hours at a time, so that the teacher may be sure he is listening or studying books. Short periods of exercise are allowed as a bribe to keep him quiet the rest of the time, but these relaxations do not compensate for the efforts which he must make. The child is eager to move both mentally and physically. Just as the physical growth must progress together with the mental, so it is in the separate acts of a child. His bodily movements and his mental awakening are mutually dependent upon each other.

It is not enough to state this principle without carrying its proof into practice, says Mrs. Johnson. The child with the well-nourished, active body is the child who is most anxious to do and to know things. The need of activity must be met in the exercise of the school, hour by hour; the child must be allowed to move about both in work and in play, to imitate and to discover for himself. The world of objects around him is an unexplored hemisphere to the child even at the age of six years, a world constantly enlarging to his small vision as his activities carry him further and further in his investigations, a world by no means so commonplace to him as to the adult. Therefore, let the child, while his muscles are soft and his mind susceptible, look for himself at the world of things both natural and artificial, which is for him the source of knowledge.

Instead of providing this chance for growth and discovery, the ordinary school impresses the little one into a narrow area, into a melancholy silence, into a forced attitude of mind and body, till his curiosity is dulled into surprise at the strange things happening to him. Very soon his body is tired of his task and he begins to find ways of evading his teacher, to look about him for an escape from his little prison. This means that he becomes restless and impatient, in the language of the school, that he loses interest in the small tasks set for him and consequently in that new world so alluring a little while ago. The disease of indifference has attacked his sensitive soul, before he is fairly started on the road to knowledge.

The reason for having a school where children work together is that the child must learn to work with others. Granting this, Mrs. Johnson has tried to find a plan giving the utmost liberty of individual development. Because the young child is unfitted by reason of his soft muscles and his immature senses to the hard task of settling down to fine work on the details of things, he should not begin school life by learning to read and write, nor by learning to handle small playthings or tools. He must continue the natural course he began at home of running from one interesting object to another, of inquiring into the meaning of these objects, and above all of tracing the relation between the different objects. All this must be done in a large way so that he gets the names and bearings of the obvious facts as they appear in their order. Thus the obscure and difficult facts come to light one after another without being forced upon the child's attention by the teacher. One discovery leads to another, and the interest of pursuit leads the child of his own accord into investigations that often amount to severe intellectual discipline.

Following this path of natural growth, the child is led into reading, writing, arithmetic, geography, etc., by his own desire to know. We must wait for the desire of the child, for the consciousness of need, says Mrs. Johnson; then we must promptly supply the means to satisfy the child's desire. Therefore, the age of learning to read is put off until the child is well grounded in his experience and knowledge of the larger relations of things. Mrs. Johnson goes so far as to prevent children from learning to read at too early an age. At eight or nine years, she thinks they are keen to explore books just as they have previously explored things. By this time they recognize the need and use of the information contained in books; they have found out they can get this information in no other way. Hence, the actual learning to read is hardly a problem; children teach themselves. Under the stimulus of interest in arriving at the knowledge of some particular subject, they overcome the mechanical difficulty of reading with ease and rapidity. Reading is not to them an isolated exercise; it is a means of acquiring a much-desired object. Like climbing the pantry shelves, its difficulties and dangers are lost sight of in the absorbing desire to satisfy the mental appetite.

Each of the subjects of the curriculum should be given to the child to meet a demand on his part for a greater knowledge of relations than he can get from studying objects. Arithmetic and abstract notions represented by figures are meaningless to the child of six, but numbers as a part of the things he is playing with or using every day are so full of meaning that he soon finds he cannot get along without a knowledge of them.

Mrs. Johnson is trying an experiment under conditions which hold in public schools, and she believes that her methods are feasible for any public school system. She charges practically no tuition, and any child is welcome. She calls her methods of education "organic" because they follow the natural growth of the pupil. The school aims to provide for the child the occupations and activities necessary at each stage of development for his unfolding at that stage. Therefore, she insists that general development instead of the amount of information acquired, shall control the classification of the pupils. Division into groups is made where it is found that the children naturally divide themselves. These groups are called "Life Classes" instead of grades. The first life class ends between the eighth and ninth years; the second between the eleventh and twelfth, and since an even more marked change of interests and tastes occurs at the period of adolescence, there are distinct high-school classes. The work within the group is then arranged to give the pupils the experiences which are needed at that age for the development of their bodies, minds, and spirits.

Doing forced tasks, assignment of lessons to study, and ordinary examinations have no share in the Fairhope curriculum. Hence, the children do not acquire that dislike of learning and mistrust of what a teacher or text-book says, which are unfortunately so common among scholars in the ordinary school. They exercise their instincts to learn naturally, without that self-consciousness which comes from having been forced to keep their minds on examinations and promotions.

Bright and intelligent children often acquire a distaste for the schoolroom and what comes out of it, which they not only never wholly outgrow but which is a real handicap to them as they grow up, often preventing them from taking their college work seriously, and making them suspicious of all ideas not actually deduced from their own experience outside the classroom. Perhaps they grow so docile they acquiesce in all authoritative statements whatsoever, and lose their sense of reality. We tell our children that books are the storehouses of the world, and that they contain the heritage of the past without which we would be savages; then we teach them so that they hate books of information and discount what a teacher tells them. Incompetency is general not because people are not instructed enough as children, but because they cannot and do not make any use of what they learn. The extent to which this is due to an early mistrust of school and the learning associated with it cannot be overstated.

The students at Fairhope will never have this handicap to contend with. They are uniformly happy in school, and enthusiastically proclaim their "love" for it. Not only is the work interesting to the group as a whole, but no individual child is forced to a task that does not appeal; each pupil may do as he pleases as long as he does not interfere with any one else. The children are not freed, however, from all discipline. They must keep at work while they are in school, and learn not to bother their neighbors, as well as to help them when necessary. Caprice or laziness does not excuse a child from following a healthy or useful régime.

Mrs. Johnson feels that children in their early years are neither moral nor immoral, but simply unmoral; their sense of right and wrong has not yet begun to develop. Therefore, they should be allowed as much freedom as possible; prohibitions and commands, the result of which either upon themselves or their companions they cannot understand, are bound to be meaningless; their tendency is to make the child secretive and deceitful. Give a child plenty of healthy activity. When he must be disciplined, do not appeal to a sense which he has not got, but show him by a little pain if necessary what his naughty act meant to his playmate. If he is to share in fun and good things with his family and friends, he must behave so that they will want his company. This is a motive which a young child can understand, for he knows when his friends are agreeable or disagreeable to him. There is less in such a scheme of discipline that impels the child to shirk or conceal, to lie or to become too conscious of his acts, than in a discipline based on moral grounds, which seems to the child to be a mere excuse for forcing him to do something simply because some grown person wants it done.

Lack of self-consciousness is a positive gain on the side of happiness. Mrs. Johnson's scheme of discipline contributes toward that love of school and work which all teaching aims to establish. When work is interesting, it is not necessary to hamper children in their performance of it by meaningless restrictions and petty prohibitions. When children work willingly they come to associate learning with the doing of what is congenial. This is undoubtedly of positive moral value. It helps develop a confident, cheerful attitude toward work; an ability to face a task without dislike or repulsion, which is of more real value in character building than doing hard, distasteful tasks, or forcing attention and obedience.

The division into age groups or "life classes" takes away that emphasis upon the pupils' failures and shortcomings which is bound to be more or less evident where pupils are graded according to their proficiency in books. The child who is slow mentally is not made to feel that he is disgraced. Attention is not called to him and he is not prodded, scolded, or "flunked." Unaware of his own weaknesses, he retains the moral support of confidence in himself; and his hand work and physical accomplishments frequently give him prestige among his fellows. Mrs. Johnson believes that the recitations and examination of the ordinary school-room are merely devices to make the work easier for the teacher; while the consciousness of what he does or does not "know," resulting from marks and grades, is harmful to the child just as an emphasis of his failures is harmful.

The Fairhope pupils compare favorably with pupils in the ordinary public schools. When for any reason they make a change, they have always been able to work with other children of their age without extra effort; they are apt to be stronger physically and are much more capable with their hands, while they have a real love of books and study that makes them equally strong on the purely cultural side of their work. The organic curriculum has been worked out in detail and in use longest for the younger children, but Mrs. Johnson is convinced the principle of her work will apply equally well to high school pupils and is beginning an experiment with high school children. Under her direction the school has proved a decided success. Time and larger opportunities will undoubtedly correct the weak spots and discrepancies that are bound to appear while any school is in the experimental stage. The school has provided conditions for wholesome, natural growth in small enough groups for the teacher (as a leader rather than an instructor) to become acquainted with the weaknesses of each child individually and then to adapt the work to the individual needs.

It has demonstrated that it is possible for children to lead the same natural lives in school that they lead in good homes outside of school hours; to progress bodily, mentally, and morally in school without factitious pressure, rewards, examinations, grades, or promotions, while they acquire sufficient control of the conventional tools of learning and of study of books—reading, writing, and figuring—to be able to use them independently.

INDEX

INDEX OF ILLUSTRATIONS